Tom Hood

A Bunch of Keys

Where they were found and what they might have unlocked. A Christmas book

Tom Hood

A Bunch of Keys
Where they were found and what they might have unlocked. A Christmas book

ISBN/EAN: 9783337062880

Printed in Europe, USA, Canada, Australia, Japan

Cover: Foto ©Lupo / pixelio.de

More available books at **www.hansebooks.com**

A BUNCH OF KEYS.

"Let's light a fire."—PAGE 24.

A

BUNCH OF KEYS

WHERE THEY WERE FOUND

AND

WHAT THEY MIGHT HAVE UNLOCKED.

A Christmas Book.

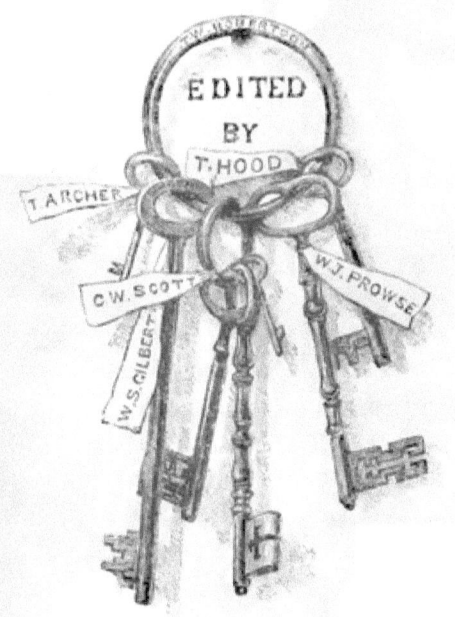

EDITED BY T. HOOD

T. ARCHER
C. W. SCOTT
W. S. GILBERT
W. J. PROWSE

LONDON:
GROOMBRIDGE AND SONS
PATERNOSTER ROW.
MDCCCLXV.

PREFACE.

Once upon a time—and I venture to think that a very seasonable commencement for a Preface—once upon a time there were half a dozen young writers, who, having to toil for their daily bread all the rest of the year, desired, at this period of it, to make a Christmas pudding.

The good old custom of Christmas Annuals seemed to them one which should not be allowed to die out altogether, and they set about planning a volume after that model. The following system of stories is what they decided upon:—

One of their number having been elected to the honourable post of Editor, it became his duty to write this Preface. But for that duty, I am inclined to think, that post would have been a sinecure.

This Christmas Volume, then, has something more than ordinary of a Christmas nature about it; for it is, in real truth, the growth of friendly communion, of pleasant chats of an evening, of fellowship of taste and feeling. It is a pet child—a hobby of ours in short, and a labour of love.

If the public, therefore, like the notion as well as we do, next year will see a successor to "A BUNCH OF KEYS." And I need hardly add, that we hope, when the festive season returns again, with its pageantry and mummeries, that we shall have been encouraged to bring our hobby out again in the procession, and that our readers may have no reason to sigh "for oh, for oh, the hobby-horse is forgot."

T. H.

CONTENTS.

	PAGE

THE BUNCH OF KEYS—THE RING.
By Thomas W. Robertson.

CHAPTER I.—CONCERNING A BIG BLACK BOX IN A SPARE BED-ROOM 1

CHAPTER II.—CONCERNING THE CONTENTS OF THE BIG BLACK BOX 7

CHAPTER III.—CONCERNING THE ADVENTURES INTO WHICH THE CONTENTS OF THE BIG BLACK BOX LED US . 13

CHAPTER IV.—CONCERNING THE GHOST, AND HOW WE WENT INSIDE IT 29

THE KEY OF THE PIANO. *By Thomas Archer* 43

THE KEY OF THE STRONG ROOM.
By William S. Gilbert.

CHAPTER I.—HOW JOHNNY POUNCE WENT TO THE BAD 91

CHAPTER II.—HOW JOHNNY POUNCE SPENT A CONSIDERABLE TIME AT THE BAD 108

CHAPTER III.—HOW JOHNNY POUNCE CAME BACK TO THE GOOD AGAIN 127

THE KEY OF THE NURSERY CUPBOARD.
By Thomas Hood 145

THE KEY OF THE STUDY. *By William J. Prowse* 199

THREE KEYS ON A SMALL RING OF THEIR OWN. *By Clement W. Scott*

    CHAPTER I.—THE KEY OF THE DRESSING-ROOM . . 241

    CHAPTER II.—THE KEY OF THE STORE-ROOM . . 259

    CHAPTER III.—THE KEY OF THE DESK . . . 278

THE END. *By Thomas W. Robertson* 291

THE RING.

A BUNCH OF KEYS.

CHAPTER I.

CONCERNING A BIG BLACK BOX IN A SPARE BED-ROOM.

"Suppose, Bob, we force the lock!"

I should perhaps mention, for the instruction and amusement of the reader—but as I never wrote a book before and am aged fourteen, errors must be excused—that Bob, although my brother, was two years younger.

That is, two years younger than I. We presented a marked contrast, we two brothers. I was fond of reading, and even at the early age of eight had composed verses. Bob, although good-natured, was not a clever scholar, but he was a first-rate fighter, jumper, climber, and tumbler. We got on very well, and were always together, but as a companion from an intellectual point of view, Bob was nowhere.

We lived with our father in an old-fashioned rookery of an house, a mile away from any other, in the midland counties. Our mother had died when Bob was a baby. Father had been a disappointed man. He ought to have had a large fortune, but somehow or other didn't get it, in consequence of Chancery; so he took our house, which had a few acres of ground attached to it, grass and arable, and went up to London every now and then to look after his law business. We had a housekeeper—old Martha—who looked after us, and a servant called Jane, who looked after Martha.

And she was a very curious person was that Jane. Why once she tried to drown herself in the Beck, because her sweetheart had proved false to her, and married somebody else; and yet Jane was a very plain girl, with a nose like a piece of bottle india-rubber, she could hardly read and couldn't write at all. But as I was saying, we lived in this old-fashioned rookery, and went every day a mile across the fields to the Reverend Mr. Dewhurst's to school. It wasn't a regular school the Reverend Dewhurst's, but he used to teach us. He was curate to the church at Thorpcroft was the Reverend Dewhurst, and a great friend of father's, and Mrs. Dewhurst was a very nice woman, and their daughter Amy was a very nice girl. No imagination, but a very nice girl for all that.

I remember the gentleman who owned the box coming to stop a week with father. I remember him particularly well, though I was only six years old—I have a wonderful memory—because the end of his nose was like a sponge, a red sponge. He was a tall man, and very pale, and wore a wig, and had a voice so deep and so musical, that it was beautiful to listen to it. While he was stopping with us, the Reverend Dewhurst used to come over to supper with father almost every evening; the three of them had been schoolfellows when boys—Rugbeians—and they used to sit up over their whisky and water till early in the morning, at least so I have heard Martha say; and I remember myself hearing father tell Mrs. Dewhurst when she complained of the Reverend Dewhurst's hours, that he, the tall, pale gentleman, was the only man who understood the art of reciting poetry as it ought to be recited.

Well, it was he, the stranger, who brought the box with him, and it was placed where he slept in our spare bed-room. It was a very big black box, and he had no other luggage.

One morning I was sent off to the Reverend Dewhurst's in a jiffy, and I stopped with Mrs. Dewhurst and Amy for a week. I have been told since that I was sent to be out of the way, for that the tall, pale gentleman not coming down to breakfast at the usual time, my father went up to his room to call him, and found him dead in his bed.

He was buried at Thorpcroft churchyard, and the Reverend Dewhurst read the burial service over him. I was sent back home, and the big black box had never been moved from our spare bedroom, nor had the broad strap round it ever been unbuckled.

Years rolled by, and I merged from childhood

into youth. I learned rapidly, the Reverend Dewhurst said too rapidly, and encouraged by my brother Bob's approval, and the bright eyes of Amy, I looked forward to a glorious career.

I was intensely fond of reading, and as Mrs. Dewhurst had all the new novels sent to her every month in a green box from the library, I had my fill of romance, sentiment, and adventure. Books formed my mind; while but youthful I was in intellect a man. Even at what some persons would consider the early age of eleven, I had formed an attachment for Miss Dewhurst—my Amy, a love which I feel will last my life.

It was so pleasant to go out mushrooming together on the common, with a book, to sit beside a streamlet beneath the bending branches of a willow, looking over the same page while Bob gathered the mushrooms; for poor Bob had no sentiment. Give him his ditch and his bird's nest, and he cared for nothing else. Amy Dewhurst. What a name for a poet's bride!

But the fatal time for parting came. The knell was tolled. The command was given! The fiat went forth. Amy was to go to boarding-school!

I will not attempt to describe my grief, or how poor dear Bob endeavoured to console me with the pine-apple rock, which he that day purchased at Thorpcroft Feast. Dear, stupid old Bob, how could he understand *my* feelings?

I went to the Feast the next day to banish my regret, and I tried to obtain a temporary distraction from a blighted heart by visiting all the shows. We, Bob, and I, saw the Leicestershire giant, the pink-eyed Albino lady with the long white hair, the boa constrictor, and the armadillo, the battle of Navarino, and the siege of Seringapatam, an Indian chieftain fresh from his native wilds, and a small circus, with some capital tumbling by the Professors Diavolini. I thought the circus performance would have driven Bob mad. He did nothing but tumble and stand on the bare back of our old pony for days after. I think the showman took a deal of money, for I saw the Indian chieftain quaffing firewater at the Four All's with his proprietor and tamer.

It was about this time, the sad time of Amy's departure, that I began thinking about the big black box in the spare bed-room. I don't know why I connected these two apparently opposing facts; but I did, and I wondered what was inside the box. I asked Martha, but she said she didn't know; nor was she conscious of the existence of a key. This was in the beginning of December; my father had gone up to the Swampham Station, six miles from our house, and started for London to look after his law business. I remember he said before he went that "this time he hoped to bring back news one way or the other."

The idea of the contents of the box haunted me; in fact it divided my mind with thoughts of my Amy. I held long councils with Bob, who always agreed with me in everything, but made no suggestions from himself. It was in the tool-house in the garden, and he was standing on his head when I said to him the words with which I commenced the story.

"Suppose, Bob, we force the lock!"

"Suppose we do," said Bob from his inverted position on the floor.

"Father is gone to London," I remarked.

"Yes," answered Bob, walking on his hands through the door into the garden.

"Then there is Martha."

"Blow Martha!" said Bob, doing hand-springs right along the gravel-path.

"Bob!" I shouted after him.

"Yes," he replied on his head again, and clapping his feet together.

"If without any personal inconvenience you could manage to stand upon your feet like a Christian, we might discuss this subject like intellectual beings."

Bob's body went down full length on the gravel with a whack, and then he threw himself upon his feet after the manner of Signor Antonio Diavolini.

"Suppose we force the lock!"

"And see what's inside?"

"That follows as a matter of course."

Bob crowed like a cock, fluttered his elbows, and said, "Martha!"

I grasped his arm, and whispered in his ear, "To-night, when she is asleep, the household wrapped in slumber——"

"Right you are," he interrupted, and immediately threw hand-springs in the direction of the tool-house. He was enough to provoke a saint.

"Where are you going?" I shouted.

"Chisel!" he replied, and vanished from my sight.

CHAPTER II.

CONCERNING THE CONTENTS OF THE BIG BLACK BOX.

Bob, by my direction, secreted some lucifers, wrapped them in a piece of paper and put them in his pocket. He also procured about four inches of candle, which he kept in the crown of his cap. Martha remarked that evening that we seemed in an unusual hurry to get to bed. At half-past eight she tucked us up, kissed us, wished us good night, and took our light away.

Little did she think of the project that was afoot.

"Steve," said Bob, when we were alone in the dark, "when Martha kissed us I didn't like to think of what we were going to do."

"Why not?" I asked.

"It seems so sneakish."

"Are you afraid?" I confess I began to feel a bit nervous myself.

"No, I'm not afraid; but I hate to know anything that everybody else don't know."

Bob was very stupid.

We didn't play that night at Wild Horse of the Prairies—our constant custom before going to sleep—but lay watching and watching, and waiting and waiting for Martha and Jane and John Simpson to go to bed. John Simpson was a labourer who always slept in the house when father was away. Oh, that night! How long every minute seemed, and how I thought of the big black box standing in the spare bedroom. I grew almost frightened, for I imagined that when we opened it we might find a dead body, or the spirit of the tall pale gentleman, to whom in life it had belonged; or if a dreadful head should rise up and say, " Is it time ?" as in the oil jar in the " Forty Thieves !" I almost repented our project, and wished we had never undertaken it; but then we had the four inches of candle, the lucifers, and the chisel; and of what good were those implements unless we used them ?

Bob was soon fast asleep, and snoring like a corn-crake.

At last I heard them go to bed. Jane first, then John Simpson, Martha last; and then followed another tedious, wretched time. I calculated that it would take them one hour to go fast asleep.

The hour, or longer I know not, passed, and I made an attempt to wake Bob. I might as well have striven to move Thorpcroft Church. He turned, and plunged, and kicked, till at last I was forced to resort to a wet towel across his eyes. He woke.

"What's up?" he asked.

"The box!"

"All right," he said, and got out of bed immediately.

Crash! smash! went the water-jug which I had placed by the bed-side to cold-pig Master Bob with. We both jumped into bed again, and closed our eyes tightly, as if in the profoundest slumber.

"What a fool you are," I whispered under the bed-clothes.

"What did you put the water-jug in the way for?" he replied.

"Did you upset it?"

"Yes; didn't you hear it trickling?"

"Get up and wipe it," I said, "or it'll run through into the ceiling below."

Bob seized his shirt, and the piece of carpet by our bed-side, and the "drip, drip" of the water ceased.

The noise had not aroused anybody, so we slipped across the room to our door, every board creaking as if asking Martha to come down and catch us. We got out into the passage. The spare bed-room was on the same floor, so that we soon reached it; the key was in the lock as usual, but it was so tight that I could not turn it.

"Let me try," whispered Bob, and he turned it in a moment, and we stood in the spare room.

"Where's the lucifers?" I asked. "Haven't you got 'em?"

"No. Haven't you?"

"I thought you had 'em in your pocket."

"I haven't a pocket in my night shirt, have I?" said that aggravating Bob.

"Haven't you brought the bit of candle, either?" I inquired.

"No."

"Where are they?"

"In our room."

"Why didn't you bring 'em with you?"

"I forgot."

He had no forethought.

"I'll go fetch 'em," said he.

I did not like to be left in the spare bed-room alone; so I went and returned with him, armed with the candle, matches, and chisel. We closed the door.

"Now ladies and gentlemen," said Bob—who was of a frivolous turn even at that eventful moment —"just a going to begin!"

And we lit the candle!

There was the big black box in its accustomed corner. The strap-buckle glistening in the light as if daring us to unfasten it.

The spare bed loomed white upon us like a ghost, and every hole in the embroidery above its watchful fringe seemed like an eye upon us. I felt cold all over, particularly at the feet.

"Now, Steve, go it!" said Bob.

"Bob," I suggested, "let's toss up for it."

"For what?"

"To see who is to do it!"

"Do what?"

"Open the—it—I mean."

"We haven't got any coppers."

"Then let's pull hairs for it." And we each pulled a hair out of our heads—an invention of mine which we always adopted when straws and grass were not available—Bob having pulled out the shorter hair lost.

I held the candle while he unbuckled the strap as cool as an ostler.

"Mind you don't make a noise," I whispered.

Bob took the chisel; I shut my eyes tight, heard a slight sound—"All right" from Bob—and the deed was done!

The box was open!

A newspaper was spread upon the top of the contents. We pulled it aside, and the first things we saw were—

Three swords!

1. One long thin one, with a dark blue steel handle, and mountings.

2. One broader one, with a white handle and a gold cross hilt.

3. A short broad sword in a red and gold scabbard, which I knew at once to be the sort of sword used by the ancient Romans. (Confound 'em!)

"Hurra!" shouted Bob, in a whisper, as we each drew a weapon and waved it over our heads.

Think of finding three swords—not one, but *three!* Robinson Crusoe was not more delighted when he discovered the barrel of gunpowder on the wreck. We continued our search.

The next thing we took out was a lot of garments tied up together in a sort of towel. We opened the packet and found—

1. A tiger-skin.
2. A white shirt, with gold fringe at the ends, no arms, but brass ornaments all over it.
3. A pink under-shirt, and long stockings coming up to the waist.
4. Three or four gold chains, a pair of sandals (ancient Romans), a Bird of Paradise, cut in half, and a book of the play of "Pizarro, or the Spaniards in Peru," by Brinsley Sheridan.

We next found a beautiful Turkish dress, which we afterwards were told was the dress of Othello, the Moor of Venice, and a Scotch dress, for Macbeth, and a dress for the crook-backed tyrant Richard the Third, and Hamlet's dress, all black, and a hat to match, exactly like the feathers on a hearse, and a dagger, and several other things needless to mention, besides a lot of play-books, and half an old letter. In the letter it said—

"MY DEAR SIR,—I agree to your terms; and we will, if it suit you, commence on the 17th, which will give us Monday, Tuesday, and Wednesday for Coventry; Thursday and Friday for Worcester; thus leaving the Saturday for you at Birmingham, if you can so arrange it. With regard to——"

And the letter said no more.

Bob and I each put on a hat and feathers,

drew a sword and danced with joy till we were out of breath. We then fought a combat, carefully avoiding hitting the swords together for fear of making a noise.

I looked to the candle, which we had placed in the fire-place, and saw that there was not more than an inch left. We hastily returned our new-found treasures, all but the swords and the dagger—those we would not part with—to the box, and after a difficulty, for we could not pack well, got the lid down, and the strap buckled tightly over it. The hasp of the lock, though broken, looked all right, and with a sword on each shoulder and the dagger in my teeth, like Robinson Crusoe with his two guns, I crept back to bed, followed by Bob.

CHAPTER III.

CONCERNING THE ADVENTURES INTO WHICH THE CONTENTS OF THE BIG BLACK BOX LED US.

THE next few days we employed in secretly carrying the chief part of our treasures to the cave. The cave had formerly been a cow-shed; in fact, it was an abandoned and deserted cow-shed. We kept no cow, but were supplied by John Simpson's brindle. And it was in the cave that we smoked bits of cane, and prepared merry-devils for the fifth of November. We had splendid days in the cave with our swords and our new dresses. Bob used to be

Macduff, and I Macbeth. I was King Richard, and
Bob the Earl of Richmond. Hamlet and Shylock we
never cared about. I used to like to play the
tyrant and to die, at the same time I always wished
to be the conqueror too. If I could, I would have
been both victor and vanquished, which the Reverend Dewhurst has since told me was a thoroughly
tragic dramatic aspiration. At last, tired of taking
it from books, I invented a new play out of my own
head. The idea came upon me all at once without
thinking—thoughts always do come upon me in
that way, which is indeed the distinguishing difference between me and Bob, who never has ideas,
but who is a very good fellow, and always ready to
follow where superior intellect may lead. My new
idea was to act the savage and his keeper—Bob,
being stupid, to be the savage; and I, being intellectual, the keeper. I dressed up Bob in the white
Turkish trousers (tucking them up to make them
short enough), in the white shirt with the gold
fringes, the tiger skin over his shoulders, and the
birds of paradise, which were stuck into a gold band,
upon his head. Thus attired, Bob used to tumble
and knock himself about, as we had seen the wild
Indian at Thorpcroft Feast. Bob had a large
chain round his neck, which I held at one end, and
armed with a whip, with which I frequently threatened, and sometimes used upon him, often saying,
" Back, sir!" " Ah! Dare you?" made him crouch
and go through his performance.

It was ten nights after opening the box, and

Bob and I were in bed—Bob fast asleep, and I grasping the trusty dagger which I ever kept beneath my midnight pillow—when another thought flashed across me. I immediately nudged Bob, who, selfish fellow, was a long time before he would awake sufficiently to understand me, and said to him—

"Bob, suppose we were to run away for a week or a fortnight, and get money as the men did at the Feast, by being wild Indian and keeper?"

Bob's reply was "Um-glumps!"

But I soon made him hear and understand, to the best of his capacity.

"We should get plenty of money," I said, "see life, and the country, enjoy adventures, and get back home again before father returns from London. Eh? brave Alonzo de Molina, what sayest thou?

"Tellyinthebornig," muttered my unworthy brother, and went to sleep again.

The next day I talked him over, and we discussed —that is, I talked and he listened—the plan of the campaign. I have forgotten to mention that I had an excellent voice, and was a first-rate sentimental singer and reciter, and, as I said, between my songs and recitations and his wild Indian, we could not want. We scraped together four-and-ninepence in cash, Bob conveyed my best suit to the cave, and two nights after, when Martha, John Simpson, and Jane had gone to bed, we slipped the lock of our front door—it was a cold, bright, green moonlight night—and ran to the cave, attired ourselves, and—the world was before us!

We walked all night across country, in order to get as far away as we could from Martha and Thorpcroft. We were both in high spirits, having a bottle of beer, which the poor Indian, with untutored mind, carried in a sling.

About ten o'clock the next morning, being both very hungry, I went into a village—I have not the slightest notion where it was—and bought, at a shop where they seemed to sell everything, a loaf of bread, a pound of cheese, and a half pound of salt. I then went to the public-house—it was the sign of the Plough—and bought a pint and a half of beer. People asked me questions, but I was too much for them—I had not read the "Arabian Nights" for nothing—and when I returned to Bob, whom I had left in a hollow tree, like Orson, I found him crying.

I reproached him with his unmanliness, and consoled him with the bread and cheese, which we were so greedy as to eat all up. After our repast, we went to sleep in each other's arms. We always used to lie back to back when we were in bed at home.

I don't know how long we slept, but when we awoke it was still daylight. We were hungry again, and quarrelled about the bread and cheese we had eaten before we slept. We walked for three hours, still across country, and we saw the smoke from the chimneys of another village, or town. It was quite dark when we reached it. I bought some more bread and cheese at a little shop, and then I found we had only two shillings and a halfpenny left, so when Bob had refreshed himself I said to him it was high time we should begin to exhibit. I pulled the chain out of Bob's pocket—he had on his own trousers under the Turkish ones—and fastened him up.

From a field, we scrambled through a hedge, and dropped down into a main road, passed through a turnpike, and went down hill towards the town. A stream of light came from the open door of a public-house, and I heard men talking within.

"Now, Bob," I said, "now is the time, remember to growl and snatch when I pull at the chain."

I walked boldly in, leaving Bob outside, and I found from a dozen to twenty men seated on a settle round a large fireplace smoking and drinking. They were all talking, but when they saw me they left off.

"Gentlemen," I said, taking off my cap—they were very common men, navigators or something of that sort, but I said gentlemen to please them—"would you like to see the wild Indian which I have just brought from Liverpool?"

"Three or four of them said, "What, lad?" and I repeated my question.

"What wild Indian?" asked one very big man, whom the others called Joe.

The men grinned and said, "Oh ay, lad, bring him in."

2

I went out, cracked my whip, and led Bob in by the chain.

"This is the wild Indian, gentlemen," I said. "He is of the tribe of Delaware, and he answers to the name of Uncas. He was a chieftain in his own tribe, and was known upon the war-trail as the Artful Panther. Back, sir!"

I raised my whip, for Uncas, the Artful Panther of the tribe of Delaware advanced towards me, grinning with cannibalical intent, but a skilful cut of the whip upon the shoulders where it didn't hurt, subdued him, and he shrank back dismayed.

The men laughed loudly; the landlady, a very stout woman, and a servant a trifle stouter came in.

"Lard, bless the byes," said the landlady, "can you do owt else?"

"If it is your pleasure, madam," I said, for I saw the glibness of my tongue had struck her, "I will make him go through the whole of his performance. Come, sir. Come!"

The Artful Panther uttered the Indian exclamation, "Gurr," and again showed signs of disobedience, but I was not to be trifled with, and beat him. Having brought him to reason, he stood upon his head, tumbled, threw hand-springs, picked up a sixpence with his mouth, and finished by throwing himself in a posture of humility at the feet of the master who stood pointing gracefully at him with his whip.

The spectators laughed and applauded, gave us

both beer, and the man they called for asked me if the Indian wasn't a very wild un?

"Oh, very wild, indeed, sir," I replied.

"You must have had a deal of trouble to tame him," continued he.

"A very great deal, sir; he's only just fresh caught."

At which there was another laugh.

"What did you say his name was?" asked Joe.

"Uncas, or the Artful Panther."

"Artful pansion?" said the landlady, and the men laughed again.

"You didn't larn to talk as you talk 'mong the Injuns, I expect," said Joe.

"No sir," I answered.

"And how is it, my pretty boy, as you are a goin' about the country this how with your Injun?" asked the landlady.

"Expees they're on the road, mother," said a light-haired, blue-eyed young man.

"On the road or not, Bill Gostelow, they're where they've no bisness to be," said the woman. "Who's your father and mother, my bye?"

"I have no mother," said I.

"Tak a drup more beer," said the giant Joe, "and the Injun too, thof he is such a wild bird."

"Thank you, sir, I never allow him to drink beer, it might fly to his blood."

At which there was another roar of laughter.

"And where's your father?" asked the landlady.

"He," I answered, " is far, far away !"

" Come, missus, don't ask the lad more questions; it's no bisness o' yourn," said the woman's husband. " See, lad, can you do owt else ?"

"The Indian Uncas," I said, "has concluded his performances, but, ladies and gentlemen, with your kind permission, I will sing you a sentimental song."

This proposal was received with great favour, and Uncas or Bob being accommodated with a corner to crouch in, and a bone of shoulder of mutton for the gratification of his ferocious native instincts, I sang " Isabel," which was one of my best musical performances.

I was loudly applauded, and the young man, Bill Gostelow, laid his head upon the wooden table before him and sobbed audibly. His mates told him to cheer up, and the servant girl whispered to me that Bill's sweetheart had proved false to him, and gone off with a recruiting sergeant, and from the servant girl's look and manner I thought that she felt she would like to console Bill Gostelow.

I sang more songs, and at last the giant Joe said, "Now, mates, these here byes can't do this for nothin'. They got their livin' to get as well as us, so I shall go round with the hat: and, recollect, as they've done all their work, and there ain't no " sub."

A collection was made, and the sum of three shillings and fourpence, all in coppers, was handed to us.

"Mother," said big Joe to the landlady, "I'm goin' down to the "Chequers" to see Jim Crosbie, and I'll take these two byes wi' me, p'raps they'll make a trifle more there. Now," turning to me, "will you swear your affidavy as that there wild Injun o' yourn won't hurt me?"

"I'll take care he don't hurt you, sir," I said, grasping my whip.

"You'll be responsible for me," said Joe, "for I've a wife and family; and if he kills and eats me, what'll become on 'em?"

So Joe took us to the "Chequers," which was a larger public-house than the one we had left, and full of navigators, and their wives and sweethearts; and Uncas performed again, and I sang several songs; and we made eight shillings and tenpence, and we went to bed thoroughly tired, in a little bed-room which the landlady, at Joe's request, let to us.

We slept till four o'clock in the afternoon of the next day, and took our breakfast at the same time that the landlord and landlady took their tea. Before we left I asked the landlady what we owed her, and she said a shilling, sixpence for our suppers and sixpence for our breakfasts.

"Then there is the bed," I said.

"Never mind that," was her reply; "we don't charge poor little boys like you for beds."

I mentioned this to Uncas or Bob, and asked him whether he did not think it rather rude of her.

"No," said Bob, "I think it was very kind."

I pointed out to him that we had plenty of money to pay with, but he only answered by proposing toffy at a sweet-stuff shop; but I reminded him that an Indian chieftain should not think of toffy, that a raw fowl, or the flesh of an opossum with the skin torn off its back, was the mildest refreshment he could think of.

"Oh, bother!" answered Bob, "I dare say Indian chieftains eat sweet-stuff when they're young, fast enough."

We were now in the gas-lighted streets, and a crowd soon gathered round us. I secured Bob by his chain, and made in the direction that had been pointed out to me for the "Crown and Anchor," the "Commercial and Family Hotel" it was called.

I asked to be allowed to exhibit in the parlour, but a very proud young lady behind a glass bar would not hear of it, and a waiter, a tall, insolent beast, pushed me from the door, and threatened to send for a constable. I felt I could have killed him, for the little boys about yelled and hooted us.

My spirits were low for the whole evening. We exhibited in two very humble public-houses; but we only made two shillings altogether. We got a bed at a washerwoman's, and slept in the same room with her mangle, and the mangle seemed to fascinate the Indian Bob, who would insist on getting out of bed to turn it. I explained to the woman that this being the first civilized mechanical contrivance he had seen connected with the washing of linen, his curiosity was natural. I could not help smarting under the humiliation and outrage we had suffered from that brute of a waiter; and indeed during the whole of our adventures it was singular that whenever we went to a big hotel frequented by tradesmen we were always scouted or treated uncivilly; whereas at a roadside public-house, where labourers and those sort of people were drinking, we were welcomed and rewarded.

After this manner several days passed away, and we heard nothing of any offer at pursuit either by Martha or by the Reverend Dewhurst. Twice we were questioned by rural policemen, with swords by their sides, as to who we were; but the answers I gave were considered satisfactory. I always said I was an orphan, and that Bob was an Indian boy, the property of my late father, who had long lived in America, and the sole remains of the wreck of our former fortunes.

The weather grew very cold, and the snow came down in large flakes. The cold was a peculiar sort of cold, too. It wasn't in the snow but in the wind. No matter how fast we walked the red stuff Bob had upon his face and arms—the same stuff used by the ploughmen on Plough Monday—never came off from perspiration. We got enough money just to live upon, but we never did so well as on the first day. We discovered that cold boiled bacon was a better investment than cheese. We stopped one whole day in one place to get Bob's Rolla's shirt and Othello's Turkish trousers washed. There was great fun made by the woman about washing the gold fringe, which never looked well afterwards.

We reached a little village, which was all excitement on account of the holding of a County Court, and a great case between the parish clerk and a Quaker about the non-payment of a sum of sixpence yearly, which the Quaker would not pay because it went against his conscience to pay it; and the parish clerk would not go without, because it went against his conscience to go without it. Nobody would listen to us, and we went away sadly with only tenpence left in our pockets.

We were told of another village, five miles off, but the country all about was white, and we missed our way trying for a short cut. The snow came down furiously, and the wind cut us like a knife. We wandered and wandered about till sundown, then till dark, and we began to cry bitterly; for I thought of home, and Martha, and Mrs. Dewhurst, and Amy, and I reproached Bob— in his nasty ugly white dress and his brown face— for having persuaded me to run away from them.

At last we saw a light and made for it. We found a large farm-house all by itself, with stone posts and chains before it, and at the gate stood an elderly man, without a handkerchief round his neck, and no hat on. He had a very red face and wild eyes, and he was talking loudly to himself.

We asked him if he would witness our performance; but he swore at us terribly, said we were a couple of young vagrants who wanted to set fire to his stacks, and that he would set his dogs on us and worry us; and he went away, and we heard the clanking of chains and the barking of six or eight large dogs, and we ran as hard as our legs could carry us.

We paused at last, when out of hearing of the dogs, and looked around. We could hardly see a yard before us for the drifting snow, and the wind howled about us madly.

We plodded on, our feet sinking deep at every step. Bob walked first, and I trod in the foot-prints he made. There was an odd, cold, fresh smell in the air. We were alone, upon a sort of heath, going up a hill, and the wind grew colder and colder. Our feet began to freeze, and our limbs to grow numb. I had ceased to weep, and Bob kept turning his head back, and saying as well as he could through mouthfuls of snow, that if we kept walking on we must come out somewhere.

The cold grew more and more intense as we toiled on, and Bob in his white dress seemed to mingle with the falling flakes, when suddenly I heard a sharp cry, and he sank from my sight!

I threw myself flat upon my face. Bob had perished! My gallant, generous, noble brother was no more!

And by my act. But for my persuasions, he would never have started on this despicable adventure, and could never have fallen into the ravine where he lay stiff and dead.

Oh, the supreme bitterness of those moments! Oh, the agonies of self-reproach! Oh, my dear, dear home, my kind father, and the Dewhursts, why did I leave you?—why did I ever open the big, black box in the spare bed-room?—why had I ever been born?

All these thoughts rushed through my aching brain as I lay sobbing, the snow falling over and covering me like a shroud.

The wind swooped and howled with the savage triumph of a fiend, and such was the disordered state of my intellect that I thought it roared my name.

"St - e - e - e - ve!"

I felt that I could contend no more, but should die upon that frozen bed.

Again the wind howled—

"St - e - e - e - ve!"

No! not the wind. Bob! It was Bob's voice! Bob's!

I was on my feet in an instant. I placed my hands before my mouth trumpet-wise and roared out—

"B - o - b!"

His voice, coming from where I could not guess—though it sounded as from a deep well—answered—

"St - e - ve!"

"Wh - e - re?"

"This w - a - y! For - ward! All r - i - ght! D - o - wn h - e - re!"

He was alive! Bob was alive! I crept

forward slowly on my face—swimming as it were—in the thick snow. Bob's voice guided me; and I floundered on till I felt myself at the edge of a sort of hill or precipice.

I cleared the snow from my mouth and shouted.

"Here I am!" answered Bob.

"Where?"

"Down here! Come on; it's quite warm; it isn't far!"

"Hurt yourself?"

"Not much."

"Broken anything?"

"Yes!"

"What?"

"The beer-bottle!"

"I mean limbs?"

"No; a few bruises. It's jolly warm down here. Wait till I light a match, you'll see!"

By the light of the lucifer I saw Bob's white face—for it had been completely washed by the snow—six feet below me.

"Stop till I light a candle," said Bob (we always carried a candle and lucifers); "then you can see to drop."

"The wind 'll blow it out!" I gasped.

"There's no wind down here; it's sheltered. Now!"

The candle was lighted, and I dropped down into the ravine.

I say ravine, because I don't know what else to call it, it seemed as if the earth had cracked, and a sort of hole or cavern had been formed. There was only a space a foot wide above our heads. Snow had drifted to the left of us, and on the right was earth and brushwood. The top of the bank arched over, so that it was more like being in an underground mud cabin or cow-shed than anything else. The intense and immediate comfort was the warmth, the absence of wind; and our cheeks and hands tingled as with the pricks of pins and needles.

"Steve," said Bob.

"What?"

"Let's light a fire."

"Before we do that, Bob," I answered, "we'll do something else."

"What?"

"Say a prayer."

And we knelt down and said the evening prayer taught us by Mr. Dewhurst, and I returned thanks for the deliverance of my dear brother from a terrible death.

Bob then limped to the brushwood, hacked it down with the short Roman sword, and kindled a fire. The smoke was rather tiresome, but the heat was most grateful; and we ate the remains of our provisions—a quartern loaf and a very small piece of bacon—with an intense relish. As for drink, as Bob said, there were snowballs enough for a large family. We then threw on more brushwood, using the Roman sword as a poker, and went to sleep, the tiger-skin serving for a quilt.

I woke before Bob; our fire was out. I looked upward, and saw a strip of sky over the roof of our cave. The snow had ceased to fall; it was still dark. I resolved to look out; so drawing that most useful of weapons, the Roman sword, from the fire, I stuck it into the sides of the cave, and then standing upon it, gazed out upon the track we had travelled.

Nothing was to be seen but a flat surface of snow, pure, white, and unsullied as freshly-washed linen. I detected a strange noise too, which was not the wind, but more like the slapping, flopping, stealing rush of water.

With some difficulty I turned myself round, still standing on the iron hilt of the sword. I looked up, and saw a huge white ghost a mile high in the sky. It glared angrily on me, with an eye or mouth, or both, emitting a red, blinding, awful flame. I suppressed a shriek, and fell senseless.

CHAPTER IV.

CONCERNING THE GHOST, AND HOW WE WENT INSIDE IT.

WHEN I recovered consciousness, it was daylight, and Bob was standing over me, stuffing snowballs in my mouth, and scrubbing my temples.

"That's right, Steve," said Bob. "I was frightened to death when I found I couldn't rouse you. Have a bit of bread and a snowball, it's all there is for breakfast. It's left off snowing, and we've the day before us to find out where we are."

I took a crust, and told Bob of the ghost.

"What!" cried Bob, his eyes and his mouth rounding like saucers—"a mile high!"

"Or more," I continued, "with red fire flashing from his eyes, and a white cloak drawn over its head and shoulders."

Bob immediately divested himself of his Rolla's shirt and Turkish trowsers.

"I'll wear these things and paint my face no more," said he. I think I have mentioned that he had his own clothes underneath his costume. "Now, Steve, give us a hoist, and I'll reconnoitre. Ghosts ain't allowed to come out by daylight, and if this one does, and fires his flame at me, I'll say a prayer, and defy the devil and all his works."

Bob, who had an invincible spirit, was soon out at the top of our cave, and he shouted—

"Steve!"

"Ay!"

"I see the ghost!" and he laughed.

"Do you?"

"Yes; it is a lighthouse."

"A what?"

"A lighthouse! Don't you remember that picture we had in the "Tales of the Sea"? This one is exactly like it. Come up!"

Bob, who had been seated on the edge of the roof of our cave, rose to his feet, and shouted, "Steve!"

"What?"

"WE'RE AT SEA!!!"

I scrambled up, and Bob lifted me to my feet. To the left I saw the monster that had so frightened me the night before. It was, as he said, a lighthouse, the crown over its lantern capped with snow, and its sides white with the drift. The wind took away my breath. I looked forward, and I saw the ocean tossing and rolling towards us, a ship with a white sail in the distance. I had never before seen the sea, and I fell.

Bob again applied his infallible snowball remedy, and brought me to. I found that we were on a cliff. On the rock opposite, detached from the mainland by a narrow stream, stood the lighthouse. Had Bob not fallen into the gully in which we had passed the night, we should have walked to the extreme verge of the cliff, and, blinded by the snow, been precipitated into the boiling sea below.

"No, Steve," said Bob, "we should have been saved by those who put the lighthouse there to mark the track."

"No, Bob, we were saved by Him who gave men mind and strength to build the lighthouse."

A voice was borne upon the wind, which roared out in tones of thunder, "Hoy!"

The figure of a man stood at the door of the lighthouse, smoking a pipe. He motioned to us to descend the cliffs, and we immediately obeyed him. He descended some steps cut in the rock, got into a boat, and pushed himself down the stream.

He was an elderly man, in a blue worsted shirt, and yellow fustian trowsers, made short in the legs, but uncommonly full behind.

"Now you byes," he said, "who are you?"

We told him the whole truth, for the events of the past night had been a warning to us.

"You're a couple o' beauties you are," said the man, "young trunkesses, and your father and mother is in a nice way about you."

We explained that we had no mother.

"Well, your father, then, *I* ought to know. Jump in, an' I'll give you some breakfast; you look half starved. Then you must write to your father; if you don't I'll give you up to the coast-guard, and they'll lock you in the black hole."

We got into the boat, crossed the little river, and ascended the rocky steps into the lighthouse. It was a strange place that lighthouse, with little staircases at the sides, and two round chambers, a living room, and a room to sleep in, one above the other; and the light-chamber above all. The light was a revolving one. All the furniture was very neat, and stowed away in perfect order; there were a great many brass hooks upon the wall, and everything looked as clean as if it had been just washed and stowed away, or as if it were on the point of going a long journey, and space was a great consideration.

The man gave us some coffee, and bread, and a herring. We fell to and ate heartily, though the wind was roaring and the sea lashing outside, as if they wanted to get in at us.

"I'm one o' the light-keepers," the man said, "my mate's married, and out on a holiday to spend the Christmas with his wife. I'm a widower, I am; been a widower these ten years; so I'm all alone here. If I were your father I should give you a taste of two-inch."

Bob and I buried our noses in our cups.

"I know what it is to lose bairns. I'd a boy, just such a lad as you," and he looked at Bob. "He was drowned in a smack, eight year sin', and I only lost my little Patience last October."

I saw that he had a bit of black crape round his arm, and I felt surprised that a man, with trousers made so large behind, could have so much feeling. He seemed to like to talk. I suppose that being so much alone he was pleased with company.

"I shall show you his gravestone—my boy's, I mean—to-morrow, when we go to church."

When we had finished breakfast, he made us wash up the cups, which I thought rather a liberty; then he turned Bob out, and made me write to my father, to say where we were and how sorry we felt. Then he turned me out, and made Bob read him the letter I had written.

We remained the whole of that day in the lighthouse, and watched the cleaning and trimming of the lamp, and the next day, being a fair, bright, breezy Sunday, he took us to a squat little church, built upon a high cliff, with a Union-Jack flying from its tower. The congregation was composed of coast-guardsmen, and fishermen, and sailors, and their families; and all the men, and even the women and the children, looked very clean and red and salt, and, as it were, stowed away, like the furniture in the lighthouse. Even the pulpit, which in my mind was always associated with the Reverend Dewhurst, was occupied by an old gentleman with a high square nose, like a cliff, and a pair of light-blue eyes, the colour of sea-water. We, that is Bob and I, attracted considerable notice, and when the service was over the old clergyman inquired who we were, as indeed did all the congregation. The light-keeper showed us the grave of his wife and son, and pointed to the inscription with his prayer-book. The names on the stone were Patience and John Samuel Strongitharm, and I read that the boy was drowned when he was aged fifteen.

"Yes, fifteen—fif-teen," said the light-keeper, looking at Bob, "there seems somehow sufthen' right in a man, as lost his son at sea, keeping a light as saves so many vessels to and from the norr'ard, don't there?"

I looked round, but the man's eyes and thoughts were quick and followed me.

"I ain't a going to have no stone put up for my gal for the next ten months," he said.

I ventured to ask why not.

"'Taint reglar!"

"What did she die of, sir?"

"Agey; the doctors said it wasn't, but it was—agey."

The light-keeper, Mr. Strongitharm, took us to

dine with a friend of his at the "Station"—a row of cottages, with a flagstaff and vane before them, where the coast-guardsmen, the officers who capture the bold smugglers of the ocean, are quartered, and which, like the church, was on the top of a cliff. It seemed to be considered the genteel thing to live upon the top of the cliff, in order, I suppose, to be near the wind. The friend we dined with was, we were told, the First Boatman, or Chief Boatman, I forget which, and he wore a gold anchor on his sleeve. I had often read in plays of First Officer, First Lord, etc., and this man, Saunders by name, really was a First Boatman, although he by no means realized my expectations.

Almost immediately after dinner, Mr. Strongitharm took us back to the lighthouse, and set about his work, polishing and cleaning. He then gave us some tea, and made Bob and I alternately read chapters from the Bible.

"I always sit over my Bible of a Sunday night," he said. "My little Patience used to read it to me, and thof I can't read it myself, being no scholard, I like to look over it."

I was about to speak, when the old man took me up hastily.

"You're too quick, youngster, ever so much too quick; your quickness 'ull bring you into trouble; I know what you're thinking on. I could read the gravestone becos I been so often told what letters was cut on it; I can't read print, thof I sit over my Bible all the same."

Soon after this he sent us to bed. The next morning, when we looked from the landward window, at the side of our chamber, we hardly knew where we were, but thought the lighthouse had drifted out to sea, and been cast upon some unknown coast. The snow had cleared away, and the tops of the cliffs and the country inland were of a bright green.

"Reg'lar strong thaw," remarked Mr. Strongitharm, "the fish must be waitin' to be catched, arter such a frost. Can you byes net?"

We replied that if he meant fish with a net, we were proficients in the sport, as it was a favourite one with us at home.

"Ay, ay, I'll go with you to make the first cast, then I'll go down into the town." Mr. Strongitharm always spoke of the town, a village containing a population of sixty souls, two shops and about eight houses as if it were a thronged metropolis; "and bring you byes some soft tack. Do you know what soft tack is?" he asked me.

"No."

"Deary me! Such a fine scholard as you not to know that! Why, I thought you'd ha' know'd everything."

We left the lighthouse together, Bob and I carrying the net. After the first cast into a small fresh-water stream, which was not very successful, Mr. Strongitharm said—

"Now, you byes won't run away!"

"Oh no, sir."

"If you do I'll set the coast-guard arter you for sure; but you won't, will you? Honour!"

"Honour!"

"Then mind you catch a good lot, and we'll send some to Mrs. Saunders. I shan't be more than two hours gone!"

Left to ourselves we threw our net, and splashed with the pole to very little purpose; we only caught a few small roach and dace. We went higher up the stream, but with no better luck; and so more than an hour passed, and we thought of giving it up. "One more throw," suggested Bob, and we threw in the net again. As we were hauling it in I saw something on the opposite bank that so shook my nerves that my foot slipped, and I fell into the water.

I saw the old man whom we had seen standing at the gate of the large farm-house, with stone-posts and chains before it. He was without his hat, and had no handkerchief, and was talking loudly to himself, and gesticulating violently; the expression of his eyes was horribly wild. He did not see us, we watched him run by the side of the bank and leap a ditch with great agility; then he turned round and looked at the water, and swore awfully, and then ran on again, and so out of sight.

All this time I was up to my waist in the water. Bob soon had me out, and I stood shivering with cold. Bob offered to change trousers with me, but I would not accept his kindness.

"Let's take the net in," said Bob, "and by that time p'raps Mr. Strongitharm will be back."

We found that we had caught six or seven small perch, and one large bream.

"Not worth the trouble," I remarked.

"Steve!" said Bob.

"Yes."

"There is something else."

"In the net?"

"Yes."

"What?"

"A Bunch of Keys!!!"

I looked down and saw that a bunch of keys had somehow or other got into the net and entangled itself in its meshes, by means of the wards of the keys.

It was not at all an extraordinary bunch of keys. There was a large ring with four keys hung upon it, and there was a smaller ring with three small keys fastened on it; the small ring was attached to the larger or outer ring; but the three small keys upon the smaller ring had no connection with the large keys on the large ring.

"Well, byes, what sport?" said the voice of Mr. Strongitharm.

We showed him what we had caught, and he puzzled over the Bunch of Keys, and looked at them with his broad brown hand shading his eyes, as if they were distant objects, say fishing-boats in the offing.

"They're quite bright!" I remarked.

"They can't ha' been long in the water,—howsever you must be gettin' into bed, youngster; you'll always be in trouble, you will, you're so sharp; so trudge homeward!"

When we had gained the lighthouse, Mr. Strongitharm ordered me into his own bed in the upper chamber, and gave me a glass of hot rum-and-water, with a large piece of salt butter, the salt sort of butter that could be churned from the milk of sea cows. I told him of the old man we had seen, and where we found him on the night that we were lost.

"Ah!" said Mr. Strongitharm, "that was old Tilson. He's mad, he was drove so by race-horses and drink. He used to breed race-horses. When they used to win he used to drink to drown himself for joy, when they used to lose he used to drink to drown himself for aggravation. He's a bad old lot! He used to thrash his grooms when he was savage, and after his wife, she was a real lady, a real gentleman's daughter, ran away from him; he beat a stable-boy that cruel that he killed him, and old Tilson was tried for it at the 'Sizes. I wonder if the old rascal threw they keys into the stream!"

This set me thinking. Had old Tilson thrown away the keys after committing a murder? I looked for a blood stain on the bunch, but there was none.

"Was he tried for murder?" I inquired.

"Manslaughter; counsellor Speydrill got him off. Gi' me the keys; if anything turns up about 'em, they'll be found here."

He hung them on to the end of a rope coiled round a hook immediately opposite the bed.

"Now you go to sleep," said Mr. Strongitharm, "your brother must not sleep wi' you, for if you catch the agey he might catch it too; we must make shift with him below; so turn to the wall, and have a caulk; so good—no, not good night, good day."

"And the bunch of keys," I began.

"Never mind them! Pr'aps they're the keys as opens Davy Jones's locker? or pr'aps they're the keys that locks up little byes' mouths; so go to sleep, and don't think no more on 'em."

But I could not help thinking more of them, though I went to sleep immediately. I awoke in two or three hours. It was night, and something before my eyes shone white like silver.

It was the Bunch of Keys! There they hung on the end of the rope, bathed in the moonlight which streamed in from the little window at the side of the chamber. They seemed to glare at me with an intense brilliance, as if the inside of their handles were eyes, and saw me. Then, again, they looked like fish in the dark,—bright, molten, and scaly. Then they were murderers hanging at Newgate. They quite frightened me! Perhaps it was the effect of my romantic and fervid temperament, perhaps it was the rum-and-water. I fixed my eyes upon them till they seemed to illuminate the wall. They fascinated me. The wind seemed to be whistling through them. I thought of "Blue

Beard," "Fatima," the "Baron Trenck," and the "Castle of Otranto." I didn't know how long I lay looking at them, but what with the wind outside, the feeling that I was both at sea and on land, that I was sleeping in the middle of a long chimney, with water where the fireplace should be, and flames at the top, that I was fixed in a burning lantern like the man-in-the-moon, at last I began to fancy that the keys were alive, and walked, and talked, and had thoughts and feelings as I had; that they made love and promised things, and broke their promises, and were asked and given in marriage, fought duels, went to law, quarrelled with each other, and made it up again, loaded guns, and went out fishing, and so on, and so on, till I suppose I fell asleep and dreamt dreams, something like the stories that here follow.

THE KEY OF THE PIANO.

THE KEY OF THE PIANO.

FRANZ WILHELM and myself were school-fellows and fast friends when we were both boys learning our lessons with old Father Schmidt at Heidelberg.

Had we become burschen at the University I should have called him "Dutz-bruder," for he was dearer to me than were my own kindred; than my elder brother at Frankfort, who, when my mother died, sent me to be brought up by my father's sister; or than my third half-cousin, Anna, whom he married, and who (such is destiny) disliked my remaining in the house lest people should imagine that I was her child, she being of greater age than Karl, and accustomed to the well-ruling of her household.

My father's sister, who in much kindness undertook me, was a spinster, and, in the up-hill street of the town, kept a little shop for the sale of spectacles and wood-carvings to the English and other visitors, so that she was of some consideration, and lived so quietly that, but for her intimacy with the wife of Master Schwartz, foreman at the leather-factory, musician, and mender of organs, I should have known no companions at home.

Master Schwartz and his wife were quiet folks, with only one daughter, little Minna, who, when I first saw her, looked so pretty in her red skirt and tiny white cap, that I felt at the moment a love-inspiring admiration which, had it not been that I myself was but an infant, would have thrust a fatal barrier between Franz and me.

Franz, however, had not then arrived, but came soon afterwards in charge of an old nurse who, having cared for him from the time of his birth, and being now on her way to end her days with her relations at Mannheim, was commissioned to leave him thenceforth with Madame Schwartz, who had been own servant companion to his grandmother. For the mother of Franz was daughter of a Herr sub-deputy; but who was her husband, or whether she had been married, nobody knew, if Madame Schwartz did not, and she certainly never mentioned it to her dying day.

The poor mother now was dead, and the wife of the sub-deputy also, and it was at the instance of the sub-deputy himself that the little fellow, who had a small annual sum settled on him, was confided to Master Schwartz, and became foster-brother to Minna.

The curious thing was, that as these two children grew, there was a strong resemblance between them, so that they might have passed for brother and sister by blood, rather than by that affinity of mind-growth which, as some have said, will control the features of the face into outward likeness by the force of inward sympathy. However this may be, they were the same in the colour of hair and eyes, which in both were dark, and in that longer visage and more prominent featuring that belongs scarcely to the German type most common, and of which I myself am an example. It was perhaps the contrast between us which drew Franz and me into close fellowship, for it is by contrasts that we are attracted; and by the hope of finding, in the mind and temper of another, that which is wanting in our own, our earliest affections are made lasting. My first child-liking for Minna was transferred thereafter to Franz, and he became my brother as she became his sister. So when he was to study music, I also entreated of my brother Karl, through a letter, that I might be a musician, and had, indeed, already learned of one of the band who played in the gardens on the hill, to blow the instrument of which I am now a professor. They were quiet, happy days when we used to go up to those gardens after school, and sit under the trees looking down upon the broad silver band of the Neckar flowing through the light green fields, or wander away from the donkey boys and the beggars to the Wolfsbrunnen, or the wooded hill where the yoked oxen toil up the steep, and the great dogs of the farmers follow the team, themselves looking like the wolves which are there no longer. This quiet life of study and friendship was soon to end, or rather to change, as must all the events of this mortal life; for Franz was grown into a youth, and Minna had budded into a grave, sweet, dark-eyed maiden, still with that wonderful resemblance to her foster-brother, which, though not always apparent, made itself known by a sudden turn of expression, or a moment's glance of the eye, or a quick movement of the head. Franz was, as I have said, dark and with deep brown clustering hair. In his shape, too, he was small and delicate, unlike me, who then began to grow of the figure that belongs to many of our nation, and with the fair face and yellow hair that might be seen any day amongst the burschen at the "Hirsch-Gasse."

In mental as well as physical qualities did Franz differ from many of our countrymen, since he lacked that calm which is sometimes mistaken for stolidity by those who do not understand composure and the quiet self-sustentation that accepts all things as of course.

It is the want of this which renders your English manners restless, uneasy, and affected; for the Englishman is ever haunted by the fear of being ridiculous, and in terror of seeming foolish is seldom either wise or dignified in outward bearing, while we Germans are either too self-satisfied or too self-oblivious to be conscious of what to others may seem to be absurdity in our common actions; and gravely commit with simplicity little acts of personal folly, to be detected in which, an Englishman would redden and almost die for shame in consequence of his exaggerated self-importance. Something of this was, I fear, in the nature of Franz, who was ever sensitive to anything affecting his individuality, and united to this was the kind of ability which he exhibited in acquiring any sort of knowledge up to the point of display, and then leaving it for some fresh theme. I have said that he had genius, however, which gift was not to me awarded at my birth, though I succeeded by application in attaining many things, and at length in becoming a professor of the art which I adopted. Genius, however, will go far in music, and especially with the piano, which was the instrument to which my friend devoted himself, first under the instruction of Master Schwartz, and afterwards at the Conservatoire at Ghent, to which he had an introduction. I must say in the all-truthfulness which I desire to preserve, that Franz was not a great musician—no, nor even a great player. But to him belonged a fascination, which made what he did original, lifelike, inspired; and to this soul-brilliancy he owed his success and the name which he was acquiring as a master of harmony when the events happened which I am now to relate.

As I have said I applied to my brother Karl for permission to adopt music as a profession, and he consented that I should commence to study at the same time as Franz; but in a year after that he came himself to Heidelberg and proposed that I should go back with him to Frankfort, where I might lodge near him and pursue my education under a professor in that town, until I was able to undertake engagements for my self-support. This I was willing to accomplish, though not without many tears and embraces could I bring myself to part with my good aunt, and especially with my brother and sister, Franz and Minna, to whom, alas! a great calamity was soon to happen in the death of Master Schwartz, who, falling from a high ladder at the leather factory, was so injured that he survived but five months. This compelled Madame and Minna to let their house and betake themselves to Ghent, where a relative of the family, an assistant-secretary in the Town Council House, had a brother, the owner of a large hotel, where madame and her daughter would be welcomely received as housekeeper-manageresses, the owner being widowed of a young wife not nine months before.

To Ghent also went Franz with them; for at Ghent he could pursue his study of music, and with his small annuity, which still continued to be paid, could live at the hotel until such time as he obtained pupils, when he should be old enough; or procured an engagement to control the piano at some assembly concert-room.

Arrived at Frankfort, I lived in an atmosphere of music for some time, otherwise my existence would have been sufficiently monotonous, for my brother's wife seldom asked me to her house when she entertained her acquaintances; and though I had made companions of two or three of my fellow-students I was too poor to invite them often to my room, and they, in truth, were generally too gay for me to hope to keep up with them in expenses. None of these took the place in my regard which had always been held by Franz; and the holidays of the year to which I looked forward with most heartfeltness were the visits that, every winter, I paid to my dear brother and sister, and that which in the summer Franz managed to pay to me. It was on one of these occasions, when we had both begun to earn our own living by our art, that he proposed to go to London, where he had, he said, some expectation of obtaining a handsome engagement at a series of concerts, the agent for which had visited him in Ghent, and where he also believed that I could obtain better employment. It ended in our making the journey together, and in our being employed in the same orchestra; he as an accompanyist, with an occasional solo; I as one of the ordinary band.

In London so many opportunities open themselves, that those who are proficient in their art find the means of ready occupation; and to both of us fresh engagements, for performance in public and for teaching, were soon presented. Franz, I have said before, possessed a genius to which I could lay no claim, and quickly he passed beyond me, and became famous, not only as a pianist, but also as a teacher whose connexion was growing daily more extensive and high-placed.

His absence grieved me not, since it caused no diminution of our friendship, but the rather, as I thought, caused my brother to rely on my true feeling and sympathy, when he told me of his successes with the simplicity of the old days when we were boys at Heidelberg, sitting in the hill-garden. One anxiety was mine, and it arose from my perception of the truth that Franz loved not his art so much for its own sake as for the fame and distinction which it might be made to bring him. He seemed to me unaccountably to look beyond it to something further, the real nature of which I could not then determine, but which I afterwards learned was the delusion of his life.

Those best acquainted with the members of the musical profession who are much occupied in teaching will know how often they are received with confidence in well-placed and even distinguished families, and how it becomes almost a matter unavoidable that they are on terms familiar with the daughters of the houses where they teach. It is to me sorrowful to know that there are some who abuse this confidence, and through the opportunity afforded them of unrestricted companionship, under the softening influence of music, use the intimate relation of teacher and pupil to mislead the young girls by false flattery and foolish coquetting into sentiments which sometimes end in dishonourable passion.

This is detestable; but it may be remembered, too, that there are among the young and well-born ladies of this cold and conventional England, some who secretly will escape from the restraint demanded by "the society;" and who, either unconscious of their own power, or always vain of the influence wrought by their beauty, and familiar disdainful concessions, lure their admirers to the madness of believing themselves favoured, and then turn haughtily away with pretended surprise.

I would have staked my life upon the honour of Franz Wilhelm, and though we were now much separated and lived in different quarters of the town—he near his fashionable pupils at the West End of London, and I in a more modest lodging in the suburb—we met frequently and with the same simple confidence as ever.

Nevertheless, I was struck with an indefinable feeling of dismay when one evening he came in to my room flushed and excited, and after we had smoked a cigar together, took from his breast a case containing the portrait of a lady. It was a beautiful face—but with nothing in it of softness—a dark, haughty aristocratic face, with a smile upon its lips, such as I love not to see, and with a cruel downward look of the eyes shining beneath drooping lids.

Despite my forebodings, I affected to banter with him, and said, "Who hast thou here, brother; is it a *Prima Donna* who has taken thee captive with her singing in Semiramide, or art thou bringing forward a pupil to the profession who looks thus on the orchestra and keeps her tender glances for thee?" but he stayed me with a gesture almost fierce, so hasty was it, and showed me within the case, at the back of the picture, a little scented pink three-cornered note, which he opened and placed in my hand. It had, evidently, accompanied the portrait, and was written in such words as women learn to write too early—words which seemed to mean much and might mean nothing.

To Franz they might bear Heaven knows what of feverish hope and ambitious unrest; to me they were an index to the face that I had just looked upon, the heartless amusement of a haughty woman who played with the love she laughed at.

For some time I could learn but little, and sat looking painfully at my friend whose health always had been delicate; to me it seemed affected, either by long professional work or by some deep anxiety. His flushed face grew paler, and as he placed his hand upon my arm I could feel it tremble, could see how white and thin it had grown. He was being consumed by some restless fever which would soon, if it had not already, become a serious disease.

When he at last came to speak of the writer of the note, the original of the portrait, I learned that she was one of his pupils, the daughter of a wealthy English Mr. "Sir," whose title had been bestowed upon him in consequence of his great affairs in the city, and who had married the daughter of a lord. Franz swore to me that when he gave the first lesson on the piano to this proud and handsome Miss he felt a sort of terror, a presage of what must come to him in love for her, and that he set his mind to keep himself from trespass in look or word. But she whose character was that of haughty contempt to her attendants, and of cold indifference to many of the guests who came there to visit, continually regarded him with meaning glances, and glad smiles, often she made the lesson longer and prevailed on him to stay, and by a hundred tokens, led him on to believe that she held him in her favour.

Not in these terms did he to me relate the course she had pursued, for he still cherished deep down in his heart the faith that she loved him too much to regard the cold rules of the world, and lest he should fear to declare himself had given him hope and courage.

Not yet had he spoken to her of love, except by allusion and by all those smallest familiarities which she permitted, and which none but lovers or dear friends exercise; he had kissed her hand, had composed and written love songs for her to play, had played them to her with her round white arm leaning on his shoulder as he sat at the piano, and now in answer to a request so full of meaning that he feared it had sealed his fate, and was doubtful of its boldness, she had sent the picture and the letter that I saw.

"But you yourself shall see her, Emil," he cried, as I endeavoured to reason with him prudently. "That haughty expression is not meant for me; to my appeal it answered with a smile as soft and gracious as that of the angel in the old picture at Ghent, which we have stood so many times to look at together. 'Tis useless to speak to me of prudence now; prudence is vanquished by love. And let me tell you, dear friend, I am making money, and could afford to marry, even if she were poor. Heaven! how I wish she had not been born rich! And yet no; for then we should never have met."

I broke through this rhapsody by inquiring when he intended to go to fulfil his engagements at Ghent, where he had undertaken to direct some concerts.

"Ah! that is it," he replied, sadly. "I go in three days from Tuesday, and it is now Sunday. But before I leave England, I know my fate, and whether I am to come back to claim her (so far had his infatuation carried him). But listen, Emil, you shall see her too on that same night; for there is to be an assembly of her father's guests, and I have undertaken to find performers who can play the music of the latest operas during the supper. You, of course, will come; and when all is over, and the guests have gone, I will ask her that which shall make or destroy me."

It was useless to reason further, and I could only embrace him, and let him depart.

The house of the wealthy English Sir was a fine mansion, stately, standing in its own pleasure-garden in Brompton, or at least beyond Piccadilly, whither we went (I and others of the band) in a cab, on the night when I was to meet Franz there, and to see the lady with whom he had become enslaved to madness.

Arrived, we found that the carriage-drive was full of vehicles; and we with our instruments entered on foot, to see Franz in the hall, speaking, as we believed, to the Sir Joseph who, since the loss of his wife, himself attended to the arrangement of his assemblies, in such things as were refused by his daughter.

Her I saw presently, when we went up to the room above, where she sat queenly on a sofa to receive the guests, with that same high, proud, cruel expression upon her face by which I remembered her in her portrait.

Even as I looked at her, however, I saw it change to a smile, half amused, half contemptuous, and she turned and whispered something to her younger sister (a girl of thirteen years, to me it seemed), and shrugged her shoulders, with a short, mocking laugh. I turned to the direction her eyes had taken, and saw Franz directing our band where to seat themselves, on a little red cloth-covered platform in an alcove. His face beamed, his eyes sparkled. Alas! then, he had seen the smile, but not the contempt that lay hidden therein or the cruel laugh which followed it!

Many guests were there, and soon the rooms, which were large, brilliantly lighted, and handsomely furnished, were thronged. We played the newest music from the last operas, and sometimes a dance, in which the lady (Adeline was the name by which she was called) once or twice joined, having for her partner a tall, broad man, who came in with the swinging step of a dragoon, and who, though he was perhaps not more than eight-and-twenty, had a face in which it was easy to see the marks of free living, and the coarse redness of the *bon vivant*, not too particular in his potations. Very strong and heavy he seemed, as he turned round his bulky frame, and leaned down to talk to his partner, until his tawny red moustache nearly brushed her cheek. But he was evidently a privileged person; for though she at first treated him with her natural *hauteur*, she seemed constrained to laugh at his sallies, whatever they may have been since he laughed loudly at them himself.

"Poor, dear brother," I thought sadly, as I saw him go up to Sir Joseph and smite him upon the shoulder. "This is the father's suitor, and no doubt a lord;" as indeed so it proved in event, for I soon heard him addressed by the name of Lord George.

Franz, who conducted our band, had little opportunity of remarking this man, who moved about the rooms with a sort of swaggering ease, and to me was so offensive in look that I could not but follow him with my eyes, especially when he lounged over the sofa where the daughter of the house sat, and again laughed boisterously at some joke which seemed to be directed against us, as I saw her look quickly in the direction of the orchestra.

Presently some of the guests asked her to play to them on the piano, and after a moment's refusal, she consented, beckoning Franz at the same time to come thither. With his face suffused with that same look of anxious tenderness which I had noticed in the evening when he spoke of her to me, he went.

She performed but indifferently, and it was evident that she regarded with more particularity the position of her arms and the movement of her plump white hands over the keys, than the rendering of the notes; still there was great applause, and she told Franz to find another piece, and to stay by her chair to turn over the leaves of the music. She played this mechanically, and I could see that as he stooped forward she was talking to him and that his face was flushed.

He sat down afterwards by her request, and she remained standing by his side. Never had I heard him play so well. I have said that he had genius, and it burst forth as he ran his fingers over the keys in a wild outpour of harmony which hushed the buzz of conversation in the rooms, and soon brought a knot of people round the piano, where he was sitting, I believe, unconscious of the presence of any but the woman on whose face his eyes were fixed. He seemed to be under a spell, and to translate the incantation that had bound him, into music.

At that moment Lord George strode across the room. "Devilish good, but rather long," he said, with a coarse laugh; "can't he change it to a waltz, Adeline?"

She echoed his laugh by a titter which was taken up by two or three of the company who were of the "high-breeding," and ashamed to have been betrayed into interest.

Franz sprang up; the fire had died out of his eyes—he had turned pale. "The *gentleman* prefers a waltz," he said to us, waving his hand almost contemptuously, and he came and took up his place among us, only one glance of intelligence passing between him and me as he pressed my arm in passing.

Supper was served in a large lower room, with furniture splendid and costly, and leading by doors of stained glass to a broad stone balcony overlooking the pleasure garden. For the present these rooms were open, and a sort of tent lifted itself over the balcony where we were to perform, and where also a table was laid for our refreshment, with wines and such dishes as we chose to ask should be brought by the servants.

Franz came backwards and forwards, for he had been invited to sup at the table with the guests; and yet it liked him not to desert us. I could see that he was restless and excited, and noticed painfully that he twice stole to the back of the chair on which sat the lady daughter, next to Lord George (who had taken her down to supper), and after a word or two went back uneasily. He ate scarcely anything either, which to me is an evil sign, since it is ill for a German when he eats not. Only when we were putting up our instruments and about to leave did he come up to me, and taking my hand, whisper, "I remain here, dear Emil, for a time until I can know what is my fortune, but I will come forth to thee at once, to-night; so secure for me the bedroom which thy landlady has to spare."

And after I had left him there happened this :—

Most of the guests had gone; only a few being left upstairs taking coffee, amongst whom was Lord George, drinking liqueur, and not quite sober. Franz had descended to the supper-room to collect his music, and waited there believing that presently would come down the high-bred Adeline, and that he would then secure the opportunity for which his heart was bursting to speak to her boldly before he left London. It was in this room that he had been used to give her those lessons which had, alas, been so fatal to him; and even now her piano stood open between the windows under the great mirror. So as she came not he sat down to it, and began to play one of the love songs which he had written for her, and to sing in a low voice her name, wedded to new words. Looking up presently, on hearing the opening of the door and the rustle of a rich dress, he saw her in the mirror above, coming softly into the room, and in another moment felt her arm upon his shoulder. He seized her hand and kissed it, and it was not withdrawn. As she bent beside him, he saw that a long dark tress had escaped from the diamond comb that confined her hair, and having grown bolder, begged her to give it him.

She asked him why he wanted it, and, trembling with emotion, he said as a *gage d'amour*. He had risen from the piano, and looked her in the face, fearing that he had said too much, but she only answered with a laugh, in which he could see nothing of the scornful, and said—

"Oh, true, you are going away, and I had almost forgotten it; quick, then, take off this curl with your penknife; and you, too, must give me one of yours till you come back, so that there shall be enough of romance."

With a trembling hand he severed a thin, shining band from the tress which she held out to him in her white fingers; then pressed it passionately to his lips, and placed it in the case where her portrait already lay, next his heart; she all the time regarding him with that haughty, cruel smile having something in it of amusement and contempt. Taking the penknife from him, she then cut away a thick, crisp curl from his temple, and held it twined round her thumb, while she went to a writing-case for an envelope in which to place it. Words which he longed to speak struggled for utterance; it was difficult for him to forget that she was his pupil only; that she was also the high-bred daughter of the Sir Joseph, while he was but a musician; the teacher of an art whose professors are often regarded with contempt;—this he had learned as a part of his English experience.

"Best beloved and dearest miss," he said presently, taking both her hands, "to say that you know not my adoration would be untrue; to be absent from you has to me become insupportable, since my heart is ever burning with yourself-inspired devotion. I leave the place where I have found the happiness of my life."

"Oh, you are going abroad," replied she, "and

will leave me all alone, expecting that I shall practise the lessons you have taught me while you are away. But that I will not do, for we too leave town shortly, and I vow I will not play again till you are with me, Herr Tutor; in token of which see here," and she placed inside the piano the envelope containing the curl which she had cut from his temple; then locked it, and handed him the key.

"You give me then to hope?" he asked passionately, seizing her hand and pressing it upon his heart.

"Hope what?" she said quickly, looking him in the face; "hope whatever you dare hope."

They were pacing the room together, and had entered the balcony, as he poured out a confused torrent of words, the confession of a passion so long concealed and down-kept. As they stood by the balustrade, where the edge of the tent had been lifted they could see the garden all bathed in the pure moonlight; he had sunk upon his knee, and his tears were wet among the diamonds that sparkled on her wrist.

Both were absorbed; for perhaps even she had for a moment been carried out of herself by the force of his heartfelt words; when they heard a loud crash as of broken glass, and there stood Lord George stumbling amongst the empty champagne bottles which we had left behind the door.

He swung round with an oath, and before Franz could recover his feet, had seized him by the collar. The high-born Adeline lost but for a moment her composure, then she said, "You may spare your bad language, George, and let this gentleman go; we were only carrying out a scene of private theatricals a little too far."

But Lord George, who was too tipsy to hear this sort of explanation, struck Franz a blow upon the breast before he could struggle to his feet, and caused him to fall back heavily.

Perhaps neither the blow nor the vile epithets which his Lordship used would have so affected my poor brother, but for the cruel words spoken by her to whom he had just been pouring out the love-wealth of his soul; but when his foe once more attempted to seize him, swearing that he would kick him out of the house, Franz threw up his hand, and twisting his fingers into milord's neckcloth, which came away in the struggle, closed with the strong man. Both of them went reeling against the balustrade, and Lord George was using every effort to throw his more active antagonist over into the garden, when part of the stonework gave way, and both together went crashing down with it to the lawn below. Franz was undermost, and lay for a moment stunned and bleeding; but Lord George extricated himself, and as he did so, kicked the prostrate man as heavily as his thin patent leather boots would permit.

There was a crowd round them by this time, and amongst them the Sir Joseph and several servants; the latter of whom attempted to raise Franz, but he shook them off, and staggered to his feet, looking up to the balcony where the high-bred daughter still stood pale and frightened, but cold and cruel still. "Let him go at once," she said to her father, who had asked her what was the matter; "I had been jesting with Herr Wilhelm, and he forgot himself."

Late that night a cab that had furiously driven along the street, stopped at the door of the house where I lodged, and Franz, pale, bleeding, and covered with dirt, staggered in without a hat.

At first I thought he had been rejected, and had sought consolation at a tavern; but this was so contrary to his to me well-known character, that I was filled with apprehension as he sank gasping into a chair, and I saw the mingled froth and blood upon his lips. It was not till I had tried to soothe him, and he had gone to bed, that I learned all that had happened; and then he became so exhausted, that late as it was I sent out the landlady's son for a physician.

For two days he lay there delirious; and even when the fever had left him, he was still so weak that, though the doctor said there was no vital injury, he looked very gravely at me and advised, that as soon as he could bear the journey he should be sent to his friends at Ghent.

Poor, dear Franz! what friends had he but Mother Schwartz and the good Minna; but they were better than I, though I did my best to nurse him, and sat with him night and day, weeping as I listened to his rambling, feverish talk, and heard the cough which shook his slender frame.

At length he was strong enough to go, and I went with him, to leave him safely in the care of the two good women, who had already prepared a pretty cheerful room in the quietest part of the great hotel, and were both full of glowing anticipations that he would soon recover. For myself, I said good-bye, and we embraced with mutual tears, for something told me I might not see him again, and though he might recover, I might be the one to die; for though to him I told it not, I knew the duty which I had taken upon myself to do. He was my "Dutzbruder," and I must avenge him on the Lord George whenever I could meet with that bloated coward.

Once again in London, I spent much time in seeking this man. Outside the doors of the fashionable clubs, in the parks, at the gardens of pleasure, in the theatres, and among the audience of concerts, where I myself played, I looked in vain. At last, in three months' time, I learnt that he had been in a distant part of England, and was shortly expected back, previous to his wedding in the high-life with Adeline, daughter of Sir Joseph.

From Franz I had heard but once, except through Minna, who said that he was still an invalid, looking forward to the coming spring to restore him to strength.

His letter to me enclosed one addressed to her who had so betrayed him; and as it was left open for me to read, and I was requested to deliver it, and to make known the answer to him, I knew its contents, and what it must have cost him to write.

It reminded her of all that she had said to inspire with hope his soul, of the night when she had so cruelly wounded him, of what had then been said between them; and of the portrait and the lock of hair, which he still wore near his heart. One hope he still cherished,—that she had spoken those words in fear of the Sir Joseph, and with a shame to reveal the love she bore him. Let her but so explain those words, and he would be happier, even though he died before the spring.

This letter I took to the house, demanding to see its well-born mistress, and was presently taken to where she sat writing at a little desk, in the very balcony where they had so parted, and where, during the absence of the family, the stonework had been mended.

After reading the letter which I placed in her hand,—with a curling lip and something like a frown, she turned upon me and said, "Do you know the writer of this?"

"I do," said I, "and he is my dearest friend."

"Indeed," she said, looking at me still more steadily; "and is he really likely to die?"

"He is," I replied, scarcely trusting myself to speak, so did her calm manner enrage me.

"I am very sorry to hear it," she said; then a little more gently, "he should not have been so foolish, but I pity him greatly."

"Is there no answer for me to send him from you?" I asked, still controlling myself.

"None whatever."

"Neither in word nor writing?"

"I have no answer to give, and shall be compelled to bid you good morning."

"One word, madam," I cried, "and I will say good morning with pleasure. Can you give me the address of Lord George?"

"Lord George who?"

"I know him by no other name—you know who it is that I mean."

"What do you want with it?"

"I desire to wait on him, madam, and I can then inform him of my business."

"He will not fight you, if that is what you mean."

"I expect not, madam. He would fear to fight any man except at an advantage, but Franz Wilhelm is my brother, and I will avenge him wherever I may meet his murderer. For he will die, and either Lord George or I must die too."

"You can easily use such a threat here now. You see I am only a lady, and therefore am not expected to fight."

"Pardon, madam, I had indeed forgotten. You have to me given no evidence of womanliness, and I therefore felt not bound to regard your sex. One word more. To you also this cruel deed will come home, whether Franz be living or dead; for I have vowed that I will seek out Lord George if he is to be found, and I will keep my word."

So I left her, and not daring to write to Franz any other message than that I had delivered his letter, and that the lady, who spoke of him sorrowfully, had given me no reply, I waited.

Waited two months more to hear that Franz was weak, and as Minna thought, sinking daily. I had so greatly neglected my friends of the profession, that I was much surprised to find when I got home one night an old acquaintance staying for me in my room, still more surprised to hear the errand upon which he came. There was to be a grand assembly at the house of a gentleman just out of London, and of the band which he had been commissioned to secure there wanted but one instrument, the one which I played. He himself would not be present, but it would be a personal favour notwithstanding. I had given up attending any concerts but those of the public, especially when no friends of my own were members of the band, but I asked him where was the house to which we were invited. Judge to me the surprise of hearing, that it was the Sir Joseph's. In a moment I accepted the engagement (it was for the next night), since it would perhaps bring me face to face with the man I sought. My friend's card in my pocket was my letter of introduction to the conductor of the band. It was for me to take care that neither the servants, nor the daughter of the house, recognized me as the brother of Franz.

It would have been impossible. I shaved my beard, and coloured my fair hair and moustache with black dye at the shop of a German barber well known to me. Then full of determination but anxious, I went to the house, in company with some others who met at the appointed place.

There was again a large and brilliant party, many of them I remembered to have seen there before, and still the daughter stately moved about the room, receiving the guests, as she leaned on the arm of her white-haired father. Her face, badly-beautiful ever, still bore the same dark, mocking, cruel look, but with even more of defiance, and it had grown older and sterner, as though a hidden care at her heart gnawed constantly. I could scarcely suppress myself as I saw the Lord George come in—the marks of an evil life still deeper in his eyes and on his wrinkled brow.

As *she* moved about the rooms, he followed her with suspicious eyes, and no longer stooped over her chair to make jokes; he spoke little, and when he addressed her she seemed to me to sneer.

There was no happiness in the prospect of their married life then, and should I kill him she would little grieve.

The evening passed on with music and dancing, and the rooms were crowded with richly-dressed ladies, sparkling with jewels, and with the few gentlemen who had yet come in; for they expected fresh arrivals as late as twelve o'clock, and those already there were mostly old city friends of the master of the house.

Supper was to be served at one o'clock, and I had determined to take the first opportunity after supper, while the gentlemen were finishing their wine, after the ladies had left the table, to insult Lord George before them all. His immediate strength I feared not, and if he challenged me, I chose the sabre, which I knew; should he accept my challenge, he could have the pistol, of which I knew but little.

I had just concluded with myself this, when there was a lull in the room—one of those quiet moments, something of the mysterious, which fall on all assemblies. Lord George was leaning with his elbow on the mantel-piece, and with his back to the fire; Sir Joseph was talking to a little group of bald-headed gentlemen in a corner; a knot of dames were round the daughter asking her to play to them. She hesitated, and I thought I noticed that for a moment her face was disturbed, but presently Lord George went to the piano and opened it, and then went back to his station by the chimney.

She sat down to the instrument, and, even as she ran her fingers along the keys, a strange and startling change came over her. Her face became fixed, pale, and corpse-like; her eyes dilated and stared before her immovable; her breath came and went as though some sudden fear had seized her; and then she began to play.

I have said that she was a mere drawing-room pianiste, and knew that at her best she could not touch the keys with the rapid and brilliant movement which now seemed easy to her. With a few bars of wild prelude, she struck suddenly into that very harmony which poor Franz had played on the night when she stood there beside him, and with even more effect. As the glorious music rolled forth, and the theme burst into brilliant and more varied cadence, the guests held their breath, and their talk died out in a burst of suppressed admiration and wonder.

At the very commencement of the piece, a servant going out had left the door partly open, and as she played, we who were nearest the passage strained our ears to listen to a plaintive echo which to us appeared to come from some room below, and sounded a low accompaniment, as on a distant piano, to the instrument we heard beside us. Soon others in the room heard this, and began to murmur approval; but those who caught a glimpse of the pale, lifeless face, whose eyes never glanced right or left, began to move uneasily. At the end of every passage, the wailing but melodious symphony grew louder before it died away, and as the tones sunk lower, we all held our breath to listen. I especially, who felt I know not what, was trembling violently, though my limbs seemed numb and I was rooted to the place where I stood, with my eyes fixed on the half-open door.

Another minute or so, to me it seemed, and the door opened still wider, as a sharp sudden blast of chill air blew through the room. I could see some of the ladies shudder, though they knew not why, and for a moment the lights seemed to quiver, and a shower of sparks scattered from the grate around the hearth. All these things I saw, and yet seemed to have eyes, ears, heart only for one thing, for there in the doorway itself stood the figure of my brother Franz. For a moment I thought his eyes rested on me, and I was about to spring forward to greet him, when he passed, rapidly gliding,—not walking—across the room. Nobody seemed to see him, the rest of the orchestra were listening to the music and wondering at its strange significance; the guests were once more oppressed with who shall say what sensation, beneath which they cowered into silence. Another moment, and the figure stood beside the chair where it had so often stood before. I knew now that I alone of all that company saw it, and though the skin of my flesh seemed turned to a film of ice, I said to myself, "Franz is dead!" Lord George had been mending the fire, now he looked up, and his face worked and changed from purple to white and back to purple again, as he too saw it, and for a moment gasped in dismay.

Still the full harmony of the music went on, and the wild accompaniment grew louder and louder, till, when it seemed to burst into a final chord, the lady—Adeline—her arms relaxed, her eyes wildly gazing, turned as if at a sudden summons, and with a great cry covered her face with her hands. Lord George had taken one irresolute stride forward, with his hand raised as if to strike, but something in the figure before him stayed him half way. Evidently disbelieving his senses, he clasped his hand to his forehead, and rushing forward struck out wildly; but as he did so he fell down, as to all it seemed, insensible. The form of Franz was gone, as a violent crash of broken strings turned to discord the last bar of the music in the room beneath.

Full of wonder at the cause of this strange and sudden prostration which had come upon both the Lord George and the high-bred Adeline, the guests ran hither and thither in a sort of bewilderment, with upon them a strange uneasiness as of those who have been near death unknowingly.

Pale, and seeming lifeless, Adeline was carried upstairs by the servants, and a doctor was already busy unfastening the collar and bathing the temples of the Lord George.

For me, I went down to the supper room, where the table was laid with rich viands not to be eaten that night, for the guests were already departing hurriedly. I went for a moment to the piano which stood there, and tried to open it, but it was still locked; and so I bowed down my face upon it, and wept for my dead friend.

Presently there came down to me others of the band who having heard the strange accompaniment, spoke of it as a capital effect, as though of an arrangement novel and ingenious, but presently came a servant with a commission from somebody to open this piano, which having done by means of a piece of wire, I saw that the broken strings lay coiled together in a tangled mass, and that entwined with them lay a long crisp curl of dark brown hair.

Soon the last carriage wheels were heard crunching the gravel, and with the last guest I too departed, leaving, as I thought, desolation if not death behind me. Even when I reached my lodging, I found there for me a letter, written by Minna, and bidding me come quickly, for that Franz was sinking fast. It bore the date of two days before, and I knew in my inmost soul that to him the end had come before I could speak farewell, or hold him to my breast. Still I prepared to go next morning, leaving my address at Ghent behind me, in case of any inquiry being made.

In that little light pleasant room at the hotel where Mother Schwartz and Minna lived, lay my dead brother upon the low bed all hung with drapery of white—lay there so pale and thin, but with such a life-look still in his face, that I almost expected him to breathe again, or to take up the little nosegay which lay upon his heart, and offer it me. For a long time I sat there undisturbed, in such grief as does to the soul of a man good; better feelings and holier thoughts were stirring me within; and yet as I took up his white transparent hand and held it to my lips, I repeated to myself that Lord George or I must die.

He had been sinking rapidly for two or three days before his death, I heard;—had sometimes been heard to talk in his sleep, as if he were speaking to me, and called me "Dear brother Emil" (how my heart broke into tears); had kissed his foster-mother and Minna, as though with a knowledge that the end must soon come; and near the last fell into a trance, which seemed so like death, that only the motion of his thin fingers on the coverlid (he seemed to fancy he was playing) gave token of life.

In five days he was to be buried, and as he had few affairs to settle, his effects being left to our mother, the time hung sadly with us all. Minna, too, seemed to have become preoccupied, and every day went out at the same time, and stayed for two hours, refusing to let me accompany her; but this I wondered not at, for I knew that she had a lover in Max, a sous-lieutenant, and my most good friend, to whom however she would give but little hope of speedy marriage, as he himself had told me months before.

Now when I spoke to her of him, she looked scarcely pleased, but gloomy, then taking my hand, burst into a passion of tears, and said that all depended on one event of which she could not speak to me, whether she married Max or not.

Her lover was a fine burly fellow, and the best swordsman in Ghent, for Franz and I had both learned from him the exercise of the sabre; but now from being a free laughing companion, he had grown so dull and taciturn, that I saw some mystery was there, and asked him its meaning, to which he answered only by pressing my hand, and bidding me wait.

It wanted yet two days to the morning when poor Franz was to be carried to the grave, when late one evening Madame Schwartz came to me as I was sitting brooding over the fire in her little room, and said that there was a fresh arrival at the hotel —a lady only, and her servant-maid. Wondering what with me this could have to do, I still saw that she was under some excitement, and when she asked me to come with her to see if I recognized the visitor, I knew what thought was in her mind. Taking me by the hand, she led me down the long corridor to an ante-room, where she bid me stay by an inner door while she went into the apartment on which it opened. One glance was enough: standing before the fire, where the mirror reflected her pale haggard face, was the high Miss Adeline, so worn and white that she seemed to have been suddenly old-stricken.

The morning of the funeral was in all things heavy and mournful. The rain fell, plashing with melancholy sound upon the newly-turned earth on my brother's grave, the wind sang dirge-like in the trees. Our little band of mourners, standing round that coffin in the quiet burial-place, drew closer together, as though to say, "who knoweth how soon another may be taken; let us love each other, for who can tell which may be the next?"

Max, who had looked on death in more than one battle-field, wept most of all, though he held Minna on his black-craped arm; and I, who felt as if that grave was closing on me also, prayed in silence; but still I thought within myself, Lord George or I must die.

As I was so thinking, I felt our mother press my

arm, and, looking up, followed her glance to a large tomb close by where we were standing. Half concealed by the tree which overshadowed it stood a woman, dressed all in black clothes, a hood covering her bowed-down head; and as the solemn words reached her, I could see that she shook with a violence of weeping. Till we had taken our last look, and gone away, she stood there; then I turned, and saw her give the sexton and diggers money, and they waited at a little distance as she knelt beside the grave and let fall a wreath of *immortelles* upon the coffin.

In my heart I pitied her for all the ruin she had wrought, and, wondering how it came that she was in Ghent alone, we went back to our home, where we learnt that strange guests had come in that day. Madame Schwartz and Minna, therefore, were busy, and for a time Max and I sat alone smoking, but saying little, for heaviness was in my heart, and upon Max there was a gloom which I had never seen before with him.

It had grown nearly dark, and we still sat smoking silently as the shadows deepened, when Minna came in, and telling Max she wanted him, came up to me, and, printing a kiss upon my forehead, bade me go out into the fresher air of the street. They went away together (she and Max), and I, going out, strolled about the town, on the quiet quays beside the canals, and in the quaint old streets which were so familiar to me. But even rapid walking hither and thither would not still the uneasy feelings which had hold upon me, and I turned back again, thinking I would sit for a time in the large *salle* of our hotel, and there drink some absinthe, myself to re-balance, and perhaps listen to the conversation of some chance acquaintance.

Entering quickly, I took my seat near a place where I saw two or three men already drinking at one of the tables. I had not looked at them closely when I sat down; but, on turning to speak to the waiter, I heard one of them make some remark in English, and, with my heart leaping in my throat, saw that the speaker was Lord George. He, then, and his two companions, were the strangers who had that day come to the hotel. I had conversed with the waiter in German, and as there were no other visitors in the room, this party were speaking loud and freely in English.

"What brought you here, George?" said one of the strangers; "we little expected to have you at Ghent, and especially on such an errand. Why didn't the old gentleman come himself first instead of sending you as ambassador?"

"I came without his knowledge," replied Lord George, laughing with an effort that seemed but painful. "The fact is, we are to be married in a couple of months, and I'm afraid this mania of hers may put it off, which would be very awkward for me, you understand, unless the old man would pay in advance."

One of his companions laughed, the other only

shrugged his shoulders, and as he rose from the table to light his cigar, I saw his lips curl with an expression of disgust.

"How did it happen?" said he, when he again sat down. "You have told us that she believed she was visited by the apparition of a man who had killed himself for her; but did I understand that you saw it too? It's a private matter, and I shouldn't inquire into it, but you yourself volunteered the information."

"I know I did," said Lord George. "If I hadn't told it to somebody, I should have gone mad. The fact is, I don't know what came over us both. If it had been myself only, I should think it might have been *del. trem.*, though I never suffered that way. Anyhow she *did* see it, and of a whole room full of people we were the only two. But there— don't let's talk about it. I've no doubt it can be explained by some of the scientific people; perhaps it was mutual sympathy, the same thought dwelt on by both of us at the same moment, and strongly affecting the brain to the point of optical delusion. That's my version of it; but the worst of it is, she takes the other view, and a pretty pass her superstition has brought her to. The worst of it is, that the man really *is* dead."

"Who was he, did you say?"

"Oh, a musician, fiddler, or something of that sort, but pretty well known here, I fancy, though why she should steal off without why or wherefore, and take only her maid with her, to come to this hole after a dead man, I can't imagine. She's mad, I think."

"And do you know where to find her?"

"Devil a bit—I mean deuce a bit. 'Pon my word, I mean to give up swearing and drink too, if I can only get this affair settled. She's somewhere here, I know, and I want to find her out before the old man comes to take her home, so that we may all go together. I suppose she'll be at some hotel. I begin to look after her to-morrow, and I shall let nobody know who I am. The landlady here knows, of course, but I shan't be likely to find any of the dead man's relations staying at the principal hotel, I fancy."

"Suppose you did."

"Well, I'd rather not. There's nobody here of his name, at all events; my man found that out."

"What was his name?"

"Franz Wilhelm. I expect he belonged to a low lot, as these musician fellows do; and he himself was a snivelling beggar, trying, as I found out afterwards, to get up a regular love story between him and Adeline. Why the devil he wasn't kicked out of the house, I don't know."

"You *did* that, didn't you?"

"Well, I *did* kick him, certainly."

I had risen from my chair, my hands clenched and my eyes on fire. Another moment, and I should have dashed my fist in his face, when a figure sprang out from a table which had been hidden by a screen.

All the blood rushed back in a cold torrent to my heart, for there, walking swiftly across the room to the table where the Englishmen sat, I saw the form of Franz, not weak and emaciated as he had appeared in his life, but better knit, firmer, and with a fire in the eye that boded mischief. Before I could cry out or move, Lord George had overset the table, and even as he stood there gazing wildly before him, the figure had advanced at a bound, and struck him full in the face—a blow which caused the blood to gush from his lip, at the same time crying, "Liar and coward."

This was no apparition then; and half recovered he seized a chair, and would have swung it upon his assailant, but that his arm was held from behind in a grip of iron by a man in plain clothes, whom I recognized instantly as Max.

"Stop," said Max, in German, "this can be settled alone by the sword."

"Who the devil are you?" cried Lord George; "let me go I say. Who is he, and who is *that?*—will somebody ask for me, for I don't speak their infernal language?"

"Franz Wilhelm was my brother, though not by birth and blood, and was right-goodly born as he," said the person who had struck him, in appeal to that companion of his who had been listening. "If either of you are of the English gentlemen, you will tell him that for it to me he answers what to-night he has said, and for my brother's death, by him caused in manner most foul."

I knew now who it was, and though my brain was reeling, saw that there was a difference between this person and my brother. I have already said how great resemblance was there of Minna to Franz; and now, in some of the clothes he wore, and with the disguise of a man upon her face, she was the living image of him so lately dead.

"Minna, Minna," I whispered, as I rushed to her side and caught her arm; "this to me, this to me! I have vowed to avenge our brother, and have waited long. You must be mad to think of it. What can a girl like you do in a combat with a strong man? I will explain to these companions of his, and take the quarrel on myself."

"Emil," she said, with quickening breath, "keep me not from this, or I will hate you to my dying day. You shall yet keep your vow, and avenge him by letting me keep mine. As to my knowledge of what is necessary for such a meeting as I seek, ask Max, who is the best swordsman and pistol-shot in Ghent, and who has taught me these many weeks, till he cannot blame my skill."

"That is true," said Max, gruffly; "but I have torn my heart with entreaties that she should not do this—have offered to fight him myself at any odds; still she knows no relenting, and we are here."

We were standing while the two companions of Lord George seemed to reason with him; for he was as a man insane and ungovernable, swearing that he would fight there and then, or that he would not fight at all.

"To fight here would be impossible," said Max, "for we should have the guard upon us, which is what the gentleman would most desire," he added, with a bitter sneer; for he like me desired to take the affair upon himself, and yet dared not reveal that it was a woman who had sought it.

"I will fight him here," I said, with sudden hope; "with the understanding that the combat shall last but three minutes, and all of you shall help him to escape if I fall."

"Softly, softly," said the gentleman who had before spoken. "I must say that for the follower of a peaceful art, the late Herr Wilhelm came of a family a damned deal more ready to fight than is my friend here; but he will meet the gentleman who gave this blow, if with him I have any influence. Who will be your second, sir?" he said, bowing to Minna, and speaking in German.

"He is here—Herr Maximilien Faber, lieutenant of the Imperial army, now staying at this hotel."

"Egad, if it be the Herr Faber of whom I have heard, and you are his pupil, George had better try pistols," he said whimsically, with a grim smile. "May I with you have a word apart?" he said, beckoning Max aside. "George, you will be good enough to leave this affair to me, if I am to act as your second. I will join you presently in your room."

Lord George then went out, and I would have gone with Minna, but she said in my ear, "I am now at ease, for I know that Max will have sabres, and I mean not to kill the man; but for life he shall bear the mark and brand of the murderer of our brother, and the bully who was beaten by a woman."

"I should have killed him," said I, "better have left him to me."

She placed her plump white hand upon my mouth as we reached her chamber door, and on my lips I felt that the skin had been hardened into horn, in the place where she grasped the sabre.

"Good night," she said, kissing me, "and see only Max before to-morrow."

They were to meet at daybreak on one of the quays lying near the outskirts of the city, where the canal formed a sort of little triangular island, reached by a wooden bridge, and quiet at all times, but in the early morning quite lonely.

"His friend is doubtful of him, I truly believe," said Max, "and may Heaven grant that he shall be the coward he thinks him, for then will Minna be safe, and either of us can deal with him, as I would that we could now."

"I will be with you in the morning," I said, pressing his hand; "it may not be then too late."

I would not go to bed, but sat up in the *salle* until midnight, when the house was closed; then I took my cigar-case, went out into the great stable yard, and sat down on a bench: for any room with a roof seemed too hot and stifling for me, and I had to wait the coming of the morning.

The place in which I sat was under the black shadow of a wall, and whether I slept I know not, but I suddenly became aware of two men standing near, and talking in a low voice. I could not see the faces of either, but presently one of them went and brought a lantern. Then I saw that he was dressed in an English uniform of servant-livery, and that the other was Lord George.

"You can't miss it, sir," he said, giving his master a piece of paper; "keep the main street till you come to the canal, then follow the turnings, as marked here, and you will come to the stable, where he will be waiting for you with a fast horse and a chaise. I will bring the luggage on to-morrow. You have your passport."

Quietly, and with only his stick and a cloak over his arm, Lord George went out from under the archway of the stables, and directly the servant had disappeared, I followed. That he was about to escape was to me evident, and I would there and then have come upon him, but the thought of Minna's safety prevented me. He sped onwards, and I, for some time, kept him in view, until he entered the lowest quarter of the city. Then, in the tangled streets, I lost him, and stood irresolute whether to pursue or to go back. I decided on the latter, and had already turned, when I heard a great shout, which, repeated, was borne from the further side of the canal, near which I stood, and was followed by a splash.

Thinking that it could be but some drunken

boatman of the neighbourhood, I kept on, and, as the day was breaking, hastened to tell Max of the flight of Lord George; but I knew, from the hour, that they must have left the hotel before I reached it, and so went forward to the place of meeting. There was Minna, dressed as on the previous evening, but, by daylight, less like our dead brother; she was pale and firm, and pressed my hand as I went up to speak to her. Only when I had told them of what I had seen did she fall to a fit of weeping, which was interrupted by the chimes and the appearance of some workmen, who were out thus early. We turned back again slowly; Max concealing the swords under his cloak and Minna leaning on my arm, and were full of indignant surprise that the Englishman who was to have been Lord George's second had not appeared. Presently we saw a knot of people coming down the street towards the hotel, and bearing something in their midst. At this time the diligence was discharging its passengers at the hotel; and as the crowd came up and turned into the courtyard, there was a confused mingling of workmen, bargemen, market women, and travellers. Another moment, and the people fell back to make way for the officers of police. Then we saw what was the burden they carried. The body of a man found that morning in the canal, with a knife wound in his breast, and his pockets rifled of everything, save his passport; "by which," said the officer, "he is an English gentleman of the title of my Lord."

His servant had recognized the body as that of Lord George, and had caused it to be brought to the hotel; and now amongst the newly arrived was a white-haired old gentleman, who when he heard the name of the murdered man had fainted, while to him presently came down his daughter, a pale, worn lady, with a face full of sorrow, and dressed in deep mourning.

These two went away together the next day.

In twelve months Max and Minna were married, and after going to their wedding I came back to England. But I play not now at private assemblies; and once a year I visit the grave where lies my brother Franz, and keep it planted with soft mosses, which shall help to keep his memory green.

THE KEY OF THE STRONG ROOM.

THE KEY OF THE STRONG ROOM.

CHAPTER I.

HOW JOHNNY POUNCE WENT TO THE BAD.

Or rather, how the Bad came to Johnny Pounce; for Johnny Pounce was a brisk, energetic little man, with a strong sense of his own duty towards his neighbour, and a very hazy and indefinite notion of his neighbour's duty towards himself; and it has been generally observed that the folk who appear to go to the bad of their own volition are distinguished by precisely opposite characteristics, inasmuch as they are, as a rule, neither brisk nor energetic (except in the matter of language) and while they have formed the liveliest possible conception of what is due to themselves from others, appear to imagine that their obliging conduct in consenting to exist is an ample set-off against any account which might otherwise have stood against them in their neighbours' books.

He had been Johnny Pounce for many years. There is in the lifetime of most Johnnies an epoch at which the last syllable is cut off from the affectionate diminutive as being a species of undignified fringe, which, although proper and consistent when taken in conjunction with embroidered collars, frilled trousers, and caps of peculiar construction, resembling nothing so much as a concertina with a tassel and a spinal affection, is wholly inconsistent with the maturer dignity of jackets and highlow boots, to say nothing whatever of whiskers and the *toga virilis*. But it was otherwise with Johnny Pounce. There existed a legend in his family that for some years after his christening he was addressed and referred to on all occasions, formal or otherwise, as John, with a view to the propitiation of a rich uncle, likewise so called, who was then, and for ever after until he died Something in Demerara, and who was known to have entertained great objections to anything in the shape of a corruption of his own name, and who would, it was supposed, be proportionately gratified at his nephew's Christian name being maintained in its integrity.

But the rich uncle died insolvent of Sugar, when Johnny Pounce was six years old, to the great indignation of the Pounce family generally, and of those immediately interested in Johnny's welfare in particular. They had only one way of taking it out of the rich uncle's memory, and they availed themselves of it without delay. John became Jack upon the spot, and the name, whenever it was used, was rapped out with an emphatic asperity, which, although in no way referable to any misconduct on the part of its small proprietor, plunged that citizen into great consternation whenever family necessities required that he should be addressed by name. A sense of injury is seldom so deeply implanted, however, that time will not do much towards uprooting it, and in the course of years a compromise was effected, and John became Johnny. This consummation was brought about by various causes, and among others, through the intercession of the small owner himself, as he considered the emendation was not so susceptible of startling emphasis as the shorter corruption, and moreover would give him more time to collect and arrange under various heads, those senses which were generally widely scattered whenever it was necessary to address him. A stern sense of the impropriety of disturbing the average which declared that every John shall be both Johnny and Jack in the course of his existence, may have had some influence in inducing Johnny's papa (who was then in temporary employment as a Census clerk) to make the alteration. As Johnny grew up, he continued so small (if one may so express oneself) and evinced a disposition so pleasantly timid and so easily imposed upon, and interpreted by such a cheery, piping little voice, that the propriety, not to say the necessity, of continuing to identify him as Johnny Pounce, was tacitly admitted as a matter of course upon all sides. So as Johnny Pounce he grew up, as Johnny Pounce he fought the battle of life, in a timidly courageous sort of way, like the comic soldier in the Battle of Waterloo, who is such a terrible coward until the necessity of engaging six or eight cuirassiers at once, becomes apparent.

Hitherto, that is to say up to the date of Johnny's going to the Bad, the Bad had left him pretty well to himself. Johnny was far from being a rich man, for he was an attorney's clerk, but he was almost as far removed, or so he thought, from being a very poor one. At the age of thirteen he entered the office of Messrs. Pintle and Sim, gentlemen, attorneys of Her Majesty's Courts at Westminster, and solicitors of the High Court of Chancery, at a commencing salary of seven shillings a week. The salary was small, but then so was Johnny, and it was understood that the two should increase and grow up together—an arrangement which was fortunately broken through, for at fifteen Johnny became, physically, a constant quantity. The salary, however, was increased by small degrees, as the unobtrusive virtues of the recipient became unintentionally conspicuous, until at the age of fifty-five he found himself in the possession of one hundred and fifty pounds per annum, together with his employers' full and undivided confidence.

Johnny had married, at the age of twenty-one, a pleasant round-faced little body of about his own age. She was the daughter of the housekeeper then attached to Pintle and Sim's offices, in Carey Street, Lincoln's Inn Fields, and by her he had a son. The son, Young John for distinction, was a tall young fellow, who had been decently educated by his father, and effectually provided for by Messrs. Pintle and Sim, who had managed to procure for him a Government appointment—a junior assistant clerkship in the office of the Board for the Dissemination of Pauper Philosophy. Jack Pounce was looked up to as the great Pounce Court Card, being the representative of Majesty in the Pounce Councils, and in that capacity was played with great effect by Mrs. Pounce, whenever it became necessary, in contest with a fashionable lodging-letting neighbour, to assert the family respectability.

Not that the office of the Board for the Dissemination of Pauper Philosophy was an aristocratic Government office, or even an agreeable one, as far as the clerks were concerned. To be sure it was situated in Whitehall, and the hours were from eleven to five, which sounded well, but any aristocratic inferences drawn from these facts would be decidedly erroneous. It was to the Pauper Philosophy Office that all those shabby, not to say dirty, young men in caps and pipes, contrasting strongly with the graceful crowd of other more fortunate Government clerks, were making their way down Parliament Street at a quarter to eleven every morning, and it was at the door of the Pauper Philosophy Office that many unceremonious arrests were made by showy Caucasians, who looked quite gentlemanly by contrast with their dispirited and shabby prisoners.

In fact the Pauper Philosophy Office, from the President of the Board and Secretary down to the assistant messengers, lived in chronic hot water, which appeared to have had the effect of boiling them hard, so particularly impracticable were all officials connected with the establishment to each other and to the world at large. The President of the Board was in hot water, because he was ostensibly responsible for the proceedings of the office; and as he was a ministerial officer who in his ministerial capacity was also responsible for the good behaviour of five and twenty other Departments, with the intricate working of which he was supposed to become intimate by a species of Divine Right, immediately upon his taking office, he found his time fully occupied in cramming up " explanations," wherewith to satisfy the awkward demands of members with a natural taste for figures. The Secretary was in hot water because remorseless leader writers invariably spotted him as the actual author of every official bungle, and called (about three times a month) upon the country for his instant dismissal. The Under-Secretaries were in hot water because they found that the Secretary, upon parliamentary emergencies, was so fully occupied in cramming the President, that every detail of official business was referred to them for decision—matters upon which, as one was appointed by a Liberal, and the other by a Conservative Government, they never entirely agreed; and the clerks were in hot water because they were deeply in debt, because they hated each other, looking, as they did, upon each other as the stepping-stones to a yearly increment of £10 instead of £5, and because their prospects in life were limited to the remote possibility of their attaining, one at a time, the princely salary of £300, after a forty years' apprenticeship. And finally, the messengers were in hot water because the clerks owed them money, because they owed each other money, and because hot arguments as to the comparative official superiority of clerks and messengers arose upon every occasion upon which these functionaries came into collision.

There was only one class of officials connected with the Pauper Philosophy Department, which appeared to enjoy a comparative immunity from the general feeling of unhappiness and discontent which pervaded the office. These were the Examiners; a dozen or so of gentlemen who were appointed (for no reason that clearly appeared) at a salary of £300, rising (for no obvious cause) by large yearly instalments to £800. It was required of these gentlemen that they should smoke pipes, drink beer, make bets, come when they liked, go when they liked, do what they liked, and be saddled with no responsibility whatever. These twelve gentlemen were the stock Mystery of the civil service. More questions were asked in the House about these functionaries than about any other minor topic of Parliamentary discussion, and they were naturally proud of the interest they excited. Sometimes, to be sure, this interest grew to rather too unwieldy dimensions to be pleasant, and in such cases it would become the duty of one of them to manufacture a return calculated to show, beyond all dispute, that the whole work of the Pauper Philosophy Office was, in point of fact, discharged by them, whereupon they would be much complimented in an indirect sort of way, and the subject allowed to drop for the time.

On Christmas Eve, in the year of grace 1854,

Johnny Pounce entertained a small circle of his more intimate friends. Johnny lived on a second floor in Great Queen Street, Lincoln's Inn Fields, and on the second floor in question were assembled besides Johnny Pounce, and his wife, and his son John, Mr. and Mrs. Jemmy Feather, and Mr. Jemmy Feather, junior. Mr. Feather made a good thing of it as clerk to Bolter, Q.C. Jemmy Feather was a short, stoutish, middle-aged gentleman, with a highly respectable gold chain, a responsible-looking shirt pin, and a gold ring which was a reference in itself. Mrs. Feather was a weazen little body, with over lady-like manners, and a tendency to be ultra-genteel. Mr. Feather, junior, was fifteen, and in collars and straps. He was also in Bolter, Q.C.'s chambers as a sort of under-clerk and beer-fetcher to Bolter's pupils. This fact was carefully concealed from Mrs. Feather, who had been deluded by her designing husband into the idea that Mr. Feather, junior, spent his day in an arm chair, settling pleas and declarations all day long, and occasionally meeting in consultation such attorneys as his employer could not conveniently find time to see. This hypothetical and rosy view of the real facts of the case reconciled his mamma to his entering the service of a Queen's Counsel in such large practice that his clerk drew about £300 a year in fees alone. Then there was Joe Round, Mrs. Joe Round, and Miss Joe Round, and Miss Joe Round's young man, in a pink fluffy face, and blue stock with gold flies. Joe Round was deputy usher at the Central

Criminal Court. He was a big, full-voiced man, with a red face, black curly hair, and a self-assertive manner. He had a way with him which seemed to say, " I am Joe Round. Take me as you find me, or let me go, but don't find fault." Mrs. Joe Round was a beautiful specimen of faded gentility. She was an Old Bailey attorney's daughter, and a taste for exciting trials had led her in early youth to the C. C. C., where she saw Joe Round, fell in love with his big voice, and married him. Miss Round was a rather pretty girl, with flirty, aggravating ways which threatened to drive Miss Round's young man (who was a Toast-master) into a state of utter desperation. John Pounce the younger was present, but sat apart in a moody, sulky way, that created considerable astonishment; for John was a strapping, good-looking young fellow, with plenty to say for himself, and always, on occasions of festivity, in good humour.

The evening had been spent as most conventional Christmas Eves are. There is a fearful ordeal to be gone through by all who wish to see Christmas-day in according to rule, and this ordeal is called Forfeits. By way of atonement for an imaginary crime you are required to perform an enigmatical and apparently impossible task. As there exist only about six of these *supplicia,* and as everybody has known them, and their solution by heart from the age of four, and as the tasks, when known, are of the simplest possible description, it is difficult to see in what particular feature the amusement consists. In nearly all cases the penalty involves kisses, which have to be bestowed on young ladies present, which is an insulting view to take of what is usually looked upon as a favour, and places them, moreover, in an embarrassing position. As there was only one young lady present, Miss Round, she became as a matter of course the implement of torture to the aggravation of the pink young toastmaster, who appeared to be doing the reverse of drinking everybody's health, and making no exception in favour of young John, between whom and Miss Round an excellent understanding seemed to exist.

Supper had been laid, devoured, and removed, and a fragrant liquor looking like gravy soup, but being in point of fact, rum-punch, had taken its place. Cheery little Johnny Pounce was ladling it out of a very large ladle into very small glasses, with a skill which argued an extensive practice, extending over a large number of consecutive Christmas Eves.

Johnny Pounce was eminently loyal, and there were three toasts that invariably obtained at his meetings, the Queen, Church and State, and the Firm.

"Ladies and gentlemen," he said, in proposing the last toast, "I call it still the Firm, though it's a Firm no longer except in name. Mr. Sim, as you have heard me say, left the business three years since, and he's now in Melbourne doing his ten thousand a year, God bless him. It's my conviction, gentlemen, that if ever there was a better-hearted gentleman than Pintle that gentleman is

Sim, and if ever there existed a nobler old gentleman than Sim that old gentleman is Pintle. They were good to me when I was a boy no higher than—than I am now, gentlemen, and they've made a man of me, and they've given me my old wife there (hear, hear)—my old wife there, who's looking just the same in my old eyes as she did thirty year ago, gentlemen. ("Go along, Johnny, do," from Mrs. Pounce.) She's stuck to me through thick and thin, for I've had a hardish time of it, take one thing with another, and here I am thrown high and dry beyond the reach, as I humbly believe, of poverty, with my boy here—look up, young John—with my boy here a-serving the Queen; (John, my boy, fill up)—a-serving the Queen, God bless her, and doing more to make his old dad's heart happy, by doing that for ninety pound a year than if he was managing a bank with five hundred, gentlemen. Gentlemen, this is all Pintle and Sim, and what I say is, Here's the health of Pintle and Sim, and God bless 'em. The Firm, gentlemen."

The toast was received with all enthusiasm.

"Why, young John," said Johnny. "Cheer up, lad, you're terrible down-hearted to-night!"

"What's it all about, John?" said Jemmy Feather. "Give it a name, young John."

"I think Mr. John must be in love," said Miss Round.

"Nonsense, I'm all right, father. Don't mint me, I'm a bit low to-night, but it's nothing do speak of."

"Now, Mr. John," said Miss Round, "I insist upon your cheering up. It's a very bad compliment you're paying me; I declare you haven't spoken a word to me all the evening." And Miss Round assumed a becoming pout which had worked great things in bringing the young toast-master to the point.

The effect of the usually successful pout was quite lost upon Mr. John, who fidgeted upon his chair in an unsatisfactory and discontented way. Not so, however, upon the toast-master who, remembering the effect the pout in question had had upon him, regarded young John with feelings of the bitterest hate. He was, of course, unable to convey any verbal expressions of his sentiments on this point, so he contented himself with silently drinking innumerable ironical toasts, all of which professed to invoke blessings without number on the head of the miserable young man.

A knock was heard at the door, and a drabby maid servant put her head in.

"Mr. Pounce, sir. If you please, sir, you're wanted."

"Eh, what, Maria, me wanted? Why, who wants Johnny Pounce at half-past twelve on Christmas morning?"

"It's a gentleman, sir. It's from the Firm. He's in the back room."

"God bless me, at this time of night! Excuse me, old friends, for a moment; I'll be with you again directly. Here, young John, take my place, my boy, and give 'em a song: I'll be back directly." And Johnny Pounce left the room.

Young John could not in strictness be complimented upon his conduct in the chair. The song which his father had suggested on leaving the room was loudly called for.

"Now, young John," said Round. "The song. Silence in court."

"Oh do, Mr. John," chorussed the ladies.

"For my sake," added Miss Round.

"Yes, for *her* sake," muttered the toast-master, ironically.

"Look here," said John, "I'm not in cue for singing, and that's the long and short of it. Hang it all, can't you see that?"

It could be seen, and very plainly too. The poor fellow presented a depressing specimen of a convivial chairman.

"I believe it's usual to sing when called on," said the toast-master. "At least that's the rule."

"Hear, hear," from Feather. "Now, gents, what do you say? The prisoner at the bar stands on his deliverance."

"Ha! ha! Good that. 'Stands on his deliverance.' So he does." This from Round.

"Now, gents, you shall well and truly try; eh, Round, my boy?"

"Certainly," said the usher. "'Well and truly try.' Well said, Jemmy. Good. 'Well and truly try. And true deliverance make.'"

Whether the result of this combination of forces

backed up as it was by the majesty of the Law, would have had the desired effect is uncertain, for at that moment Johnny Pounce entered the room as pale as a ghost.

"We're very glad you're come, Mr. Pounce," said Mrs. Feather, "young Mr. John is quite refractory; he won't sing, do what we can. Why, dear me, Mr. Pounce, what on earth's the matter?"

"There must be no more singing to-night; an awful thing has happened. Mr. Pintle fell down dead half-an-hour ago!"

And Johnny Pounce dropped into his chair, and covered his face with his hands.

"Good God, Johnny! Dead!" said Mrs. Pounce; "Mr. Pintle dead!"

"Yes, dead! and me drinking his health not ten minutes since. Old friends, you'll forgive me, I know; but I'm afraid we must break up; it's an awful thing."

"And you a drinking of his health!" reflected the toast-master, with an air which suggested that he regretted the circumstance as having a tendency to lessen the general belief in the efficacy of toasts, and, indirectly, in his professional importance.

The company arose to go amid an awkward silence, which was broken by occasional and spasmodic efforts at common-place consolation.

The having to go away gave a heartless effect to the behaviour of the company; it seemed so like deserting a friend in the hour of need; but there was no help for it, and one by one, almost silently, the visitors took their departure.

"It's a dreadful thing," said Johnny, when he and his wife and son were left alone. "Disease of the heart: sudden, quite sudden; dropped down in his chair, and me sent to, to give up his papers; I must be off to the office."

"Oh, Johnny, Johnny! what *are* we to do? Poor Mr. Pintle! Such a fine old gentleman, and ten years more life you could have declared to; the picture of health he always was. Poor Mrs. Pintle!"

And Johnny Pounce wrapped himself in a great coat and shawl, and hurried through the driving snow across Lincoln's Inn Fields into Carey Street.

The visitors (for they were two) who had so unceremoniously disturbed Johnny's party were waiting for him in a Hansom at the office door. One of them was an errand-lad, whose faculties seemed to have been quite dispersed by the frightful occurrence which had just taken place, and which, in fact, he had almost witnessed. The other was a tall, dark gentlemanly man, with a heavy black moustache and military bearing. He was John Redfern, the late Mr. Pintle's nephew and heir-at-law, and held a captain's commission in a cavalry regiment. The mission upon which he had come was to fetch the will which was known to be in the office, together with such other documents as might refer to the affairs of the dead man, and to seal all cupboards, doors, and safes.

"Oh! here you are," said Captain Redfern.

"What a deuce of a time you've been! Now, we'll get the will and other papers, and then you must come down with them to Russell Square, and deliver them into Mrs. Pintle's custody."

Poor Johnny opened the office door with some difficulty, for his hand shook violently, and his eyes were blinded with big tears. Although he winked and blinked hard at them, they wouldn't take the hint, but rolled down his face until their identity was lost in that of the melting snow on his woollen comforter.

"Mr. Pintle's will, sir, is in this box; shall I take it to Russell Square, sir, or unlock it here?"

"Better open it now," said Captain Redfern; "Mrs. Pintle is, of course, greatly distressed, and would be unable to attend to it at present. Open it; will you?"

The box was opened, but no will was there; and the papers it contained referred only to mortgages effected on his real property. Poor Johnny stood utterly dismayed, as he had a perfect recollection of having seen Mr. Pintle place it there a few days before his death.

"There is no will here, sir, and yet he always told me to look here for it if ever he was carried off sudden. What's more, I see him put it in here himself not three days ago. It was the day before yesterday when he kindly added a codicil, which increased the sum he was good enough to leave to me, sir; I'm his confidential clerk, sir, and have been for fifteen year, and he'd have told me if——"

"Well, but isn't there any other receptacle into which he may have placed it? Think now. Don't stand staring there, but bustle about and find it."

"Captain Redfern, I'm doing my best to think, but my head's not strong, and I've been terribly shook, sir. There are the drawers of his private table; it's the only place I can think of."

The drawers of the desk were opened one by one, and their contents overhauled. Memoranda, important letters that required his personal attention, stationery, and other matters of a similar nature, were there, but no will.

"I'm quite lost, sir," said Johnny. "It's the most extraordinary thing! He would never have destroyed it without telling me."

"Come along, you boy," said Captain Redfern to the office lad. "You can go," he added to Pounce. "I keep you on at your salary another week, during which time you be always here in case you're wanted. At the end of the week you go. Take this as notice to quit. Stop; seal up the inner room;" and sealed up the inner room was.

Captain Redfern and the boy got into the Hansom, and drove off to Russell Square. Old Johnny Pounce, completely staggered by what had occurred, locked the outer door, and trudged back through the cold slush to Great Queen Street.

His wife and son were still sitting up, talking over the event of the evening, when Johnny entered. The mother had evidently been recapitulating the chances of Johnny Pounce having been comfortably provided for; and young John listened sulkily, but with interest nevertheless.

"Well, Johnny, back again! Now you just drink this right off before you say another word;" and she handed him a big tumbler of punch, which she had kept hot for him during his absence.

"No, no, my dear; no punch. It's a most extraordinary thing, but there's no will to be found. He must have destroyed it since the day before yesterday, and I've notice to go this day week. Thus ends forty-five years' faithful service!"

"Oh! Johnny!" sobbed his wife.

"Young John, my boy," said his father, "there's no knowing how long I may be without employment; for I'm an old man, John, and it'll be poor work whatever it is. You're the head of the family now, young John, and it's your turn to show yourself equal to the position. You're the Queen's servant, John, and a gentleman. John, my boy, we must look to you."

"Don't look to me, father, for much," said young John, "for I got the sack this morning!"

CHAPTER II.

HOW JOHNNY POUNCE SPENT A CONSIDERABLE TIME AT THE BAD.

This was a terrible blow to Johnny Pounce and his wife, who had a restless time of it that night. He knew very well that Mr. Pintle had made a will, and further, that his, Johnny Pounce's, name was down in it for £1,000, which was a sum sufficient to render him independent for life. If the will turned up, which appeared unlikely, all would be well; if not, the family prospects were particularly unsatisfactory. He was thrown out of employment, with no immediate prospect of obtaining anything half so good (for he was getting on in years), and had saved but little money, for he knew, or felt sure that he knew, that Pintle and Sim would never let him want. Moreover his son, whom he had looked upon as the only prop and stay of the family respectability, had that day been ignominiously discharged from his clerkship.

And the manner of his dismissal was this. He had a few days before, in resisting a piece of unnecessary petty tyranny on the part of a fellow clerk in temporary charge of his department, used stronger language than was absolutely necessary. This was reported to the Secretary. Now the Secretary had a double action, back-hand way of dealing with complaints of the kind between "hands," (as he delighted to call them) of nearly equal rank, and the usual remedy was adopted on this occasion. Fox (the complainant) was rebuked for having used unnecessary tyranny, but it was shown that young John was doubly culpable, for he not only resisted the order, which he should have obeyed and then complained of, but he had also sworn a bad oath, and otherwise misconducted himself (being a hot-headed young fellow) to the annihilation of all order and discipline. So it was ordered that young John should forthwith publicly apologize to the miscreant Fox, which young John resolutely declined to do. So My Lords deliberated on the state of the case, and the result of the deliberation was that young John was required to deliver over into My Lords' hands his resignation of the appointment he held under them.

A more miserable young man than young John was on the afternoon of Christmas Eve probably never stepped out of a government office. He was absolutely penniless, and particularly deeply in debt—in a small vulgar way—besides. He had borrowed £5 from a loan office, and he was in debt to the amount of some pounds to the tavern-keeper who supplied his dinner. His tailor and boot-maker had for months been a source of anxiety to him, sleeping and waking; and a miserable bit of kite-flying (of which he expected to hear more on the 1st February) exercised a depressing influence over him, which appeared to increase in geometrical proportion as the day approached.

As a set-off to these claims, he had his half quarter's cheque on the Paymaster-General for about £12, and a letter from the Secretary accepting his resignation in My Lords' names.

Young John had, however, quite made up his mind as to his future course. The Crimean war was then in full swing, the battles of the Alma and Inkerman had both been fought in the course of the last three or four months, and the demand for young and active fellows to fill up the lists of the dead was unprecedented. There were recruiting sergeants at every street corner in Westminster, who talked with robust eloquence of the glories of the War (which they had not seen) and of the rollicking character of life in the trenches (of which they had formed but vague and imperfect notions). Liberal bounty and a free kit were offered as a temptation, should the war itself be an insufficient attraction. Of the starving, with plenty within grasp (only under lock and key); of the freezing, with new great-coats and rugs in tens of thousands a mile away (only under seal); of the dying for want of medicines and bandages, with stores of drugs and bales of lint within pistol shot (only stowed in ship holds) nothing was said. In point of fact, of these matters little or nothing was then known in England. Young John had made up his mind that morning that he would take the shilling of the first smart cavalry sergeant who hailed him, so he spent an hour or two in writing a letter to his father and mother (enclosing his cheque on the Paymaster-General duly signed) and in packing up a scanty wardrobe, the greater part of which he determined to sell. He left his home before daybreak on Christmas morning, and bore away straight for a public-house in Charles Street, Westminster, the head quarters of a party of cavalry recruiting sergeants.

He soon found what he wanted. A non-commissioned officer of the 13th Light Dragoons was down upon him in a hail-fellow well-met sort of way, with an affectation of joviality intended to convey an idea of what a particular jolly thing a soldier's life really was. Young John soon entered into conversation with the sergeant, and the sergeant, who was a liberal-hearted dog, stood a pot of beer (because it was Christmas-day) which they drank together.

Young John asked few questions of the sergeant, but those that he did ask had reference principally to the nature of the life in store for him.

"Well," said the sergeant, summarizing the whole thing, "look here; eight in the morning *reveillé*—up you get. You can get up at eight, can't you?"

Johnny thought he could manage it at a pinch.

"That's lucky. Well, you have an hour to dress; then comes breakfast—coffee or chocolate, bread and butter, and eggs, or wot not. Then once a week, mornin' stables; twice a week, adjutants' parade, one hour; other days, nothing, except when for guard or fatigue, which comes (say) once a month. One o'clock, dinner—soup or fish (seldom both), and jint; pudden very rare. Then nothin' till six: six, evening stables, once a week; other days, reading out loud, half an hour. Then nothing till tattoo, which in crack regiments is mostly half-past eleven. At tattoo, roll call, and bed. That's the programme."

Young John made some allowance for the gallant fellow's enthusiasm: extreme love of a profession often invests it with an attractive colouring.

"I joined eighteen months ago," the sergeant continued. "I'm but a young soldier, as you see, but I rose. In six weeks I was made a corporal, with 5s. 9d. a day; in six more I was troop sergeant, with 8s. 4d. That's what I'm getting now; 8s. 4d. ain't bad for eighteen months. You'd do it in half the time."

"Now look here," said John. "Don't tell unnecessary lies. If the service was the worst on the face of the earth, I'd join it, because I've, what people call, gone wrong, and I want to get away from this. I'm a strongish chap, and about the sort of man you fellows want; so hand over the shilling. My name's John Cole; age, twenty-two; previous occupation, clerk."

The sergeant vowed he was the very man he wanted. He admired pluck he said, and had himself cut away from a lucrative profession because he wanted to see what blood was like. Most of the men in crack cavalry regiments were young barristers of arts or medical doctors, with here and there a young nobleman or two, under an assumed name. These young men had cut from home because their relentless parents, having set their face against the army as a profession, had refused to buy them commissions. That was his case. He was a barrister of arts once; now he was troop-sergeant in Her Majesty's 13th Light, and thank God, *he* said.

All this was satisfactory, as far as it went, and young John Pounce was duly enlisted, under the name of John Cole, by the friendly sergeant. The

8

subsequent medical examination and attestation were properly and satisfactorily undergone, and Private John Cole, of Her Majesty's 13th Light Dragoons, was drafted off to the regimental depôt, and thence in about six weeks to the Crimea.

A thoroughly sleepless night is a fearful thing to undergo. It is bad enough when that sleeplessness is the result of sharp pain or irritating fever, but when it comes of a distressed and disheartened mind, it is absolutely terrible. Poor old Johnny Pounce had a bad time of it that Christmas night. He tossed and rolled about, and changed the side of his pillow, and then, when it turned out that that energetic step was barren of good result, he got out of bed, and walked up and down the room; then he got into bed again, and counted five thousand. "Five thousand" found him rather more wakeful if possible than he was when he began, so he gave up counting to listen to the ticking of the old Dutch clock. But the old Dutch clock called so loudly for "Linkman Toddles! Linkman Toddles! Linkman Toddles!" that he began to wish that functionary would appear, and satisfy the clamorous old instrument. Toddles not turning up, the clock gave him up for a bad job, and in despair at Toddles' want of faith, ticked out plaintively, "Come Dyspepsia! Come Dyspepsia! Come Dyspepsia!" This awful invocation was too much for poor Johnny, who got out of bed once more, and finally stopped the dreadful machine. As morning broke, he fell into a restless tossing sleep, which only had the effect of giving him a racking headache. When he finally awoke, it was with a dull heavy sense of some fearful misfortune which had just happened to him, and when the events of the preceding night broke suddenly upon him, he buried his old head in his pillow, and sobbed aloud.

Matters were not mended by the discovery of the letter which young John had placed on the sitting-room table. It hardly wanted this to complete the family misery, and old Johnny and his wife were absolutely thunderstruck by this fresh misfortune. The letter did not say where young John was going, nor did it give any clue to the step that he was about to take. It merely said that he was going away for a while; that if he could save any money he would send it from time to time to a post-office in the neighbourhood; that they were not to fret for him, as he would be sure to turn up sooner or later; that the cheque for £12 was for their use; that his dismissal was not attended by any disgraceful circumstances, and that he was their ever-loving son, John Pounce.

Old Johnny's indignation at this desertion was unbounded.

"So that's my son, is it? That's my fair-weather son, whom I've brought up, and educated, and clothed, and fed, and whom the Firm made a gentleman of. What'll the Firm think of this, after all their kindness?"

Mrs. Pounce mildly reminded her husband that the Firm was in heaven.

"True, true—I forgot. If he'd only given us a hint as to where he was going; if he'd shaken his old dad's hand and kissed his old mother before he left, I could have forgiven him. But to desert his old parents just as soon as he found out that they were penniless and could help him no longer, was that like a son of ours, Emma?"

"Well, Johnny, for the matter of that, it may be that he was fearful of being an incumbrance. He's left his half quarter's salary for us, and I'm afraid the poor boy has gone forth into the world without a penny in his pocket. I'd make a better breakfast this morning for the knowledge beyond doubt that he'd had one too. Perhaps he's hungry, Johnny."

"Hungry, Emma? Young John hungry? Hungry, and me a-pegging away into bread and meat, and his half quarter's cheque a-staring me in the face, and him hungry. What a dreadful thing to think of, old girl. Poor young John!"

They were not long in coming to the conclusion that he had enlisted. Johnny's duties called him to Carey Street, although it was Christmas Day, but Mrs. Johnny made it her business to wander about recruiting depôts all day. Young John, however, carefully kept himself inside the public-house, and gave the friendly recruiting serjeant, who was not quite so friendly now—that professional gentleman having cooled down amazingly since the morning—a hint that he might possibly be sought for. So Mrs. Pounce's efforts were utterly fruitless.

Johnny spent every day that ensuing week at the office. It was difficult at first to persuade oneself that that chair would never be filled by Mr. Pintle again; that the ruler, paper-weight, gum-bottle, pens, ink, and scissors, left as he had left them day after day for fifty years, had been arranged in their methodical order by him for the last time. The conveyancing clerk and the common law clerk were paid their salaries and dismissed by Captain Redfern, the heir-at-law, who was closeted all day long with old Johnny, going over mortgage deeds, and making himself intimate with all the affairs of the dead man. On the Saturday evening, old Johnny was paid his last week's salary of three pounds, and was informed that his services would for the future be dispensed with.

Old Johnny spent many a weary day, and trudged many a weary mile through snow and slush, after fresh employment. He was known and respected by many of Pintle's clients, and also by solicitors who had been opposed to Pintle and Sim; but he could get little from them. The fact that no will had been found, although it was admitted by Johnny that one had been made and deposited in his custody two days before Pintle's death, argued either gross carelessness or gross felony on the part of the confidential clerk, and added to this, he was a feeble old man, and quite past learning new duties. A few of his better friends subscribed small sums for the old man's maintenance, and others gave his wife needlework, so that for some weeks they were kept from absolute want. But these weekly subscriptions dwindled down, one by one, as the recollection of old Johnny and his distress became less vivid, until at last they had nothing to depend on but a weekly five shillings, the subscription of a stauncher friend than the rest.

In his extreme distress he made an appeal to Mrs. Pintle. He dressed himself as neatly as his reduced circumstances would allow, and presented himself at her house in Russell Square. He had been there once before since Mr. Pintle's death, to ask permission to follow his old employer to the grave, but he was curtly informed that Captain Redfern would require him in the office that day, and that therefore he could not be present. This rebuff, conveyed to him by a weak-eyed flunkey, who called him "my man," had had the effect of preventing his applying to Mrs. Pintle for assistance hitherto; but emboldened by hunger, and more especially by the thinning face of his once chubby little wife, he determined to put his pride in his pocket, and encounter the weak-eyed one once more.

The weak-eyed one was just in the transition state between a very old page and a very young footman. His precise functions in Mrs. Pintle's household were as indefinite as his age, for his duties extended from cleaning the windows to driving (at a pinch) the brougham. He was engaged in the familiar but necessary duty of cleaning the knives when Johnny called, and as Johnny inadvertently pulled the visitor's bell, the weak-eyed one was under the necessity of exchanging the linen jacket of domestic life for the black coat and worsted epaulette of ceremony, and of making other radical improvements in his personal appearance, before he opened the door. This functionary had, from a great many years' apprenticeship at opening street doors, taught himself to look upon society as divided into two great heads or groups—Visitors and Servants; and he who was not a visitor, was, from the weak-eyed one's point of view, a servant. He considered that a man's social position was typified by the bell he rung, and as there existed no intermediate bell for the numerous classes of callers who certainly could not aspire to the dignity of being considered visitors in the ordinary acceptation of the term, and who were equally far from being in the position of domestic servants, he recognized no intermediate class between the honoured drawing-room morning caller and the boy who brought the servants' beer. Avowedly a servant himself, he was affable, and in a weak-eyed way even cheerful, to those who identified themselves with the humbler bell; but he who, without due excuse, rang a bell which implied that he was a drawing-room visitor, became on the spot the object of the weak-eyed one's unutterable loathing and foul scorn.

Wretched Johnny stood on the steps waiting for the opening of the door, and improving the opportunity by blowing his frozen nose, that he might not be compelled to the commission of that indecency before Mrs. Pintle. Eventually it opened, and the weak-eyed one stood before him in all the respectable magnificence of expensive mourning.

"Well, what is it?" said that retainer, as soon as he had taken Johnny's measure, and assured himself of Johnny's want of title to the dignity to which he had aspired.

Now "What is it?" is a peculiarly aggravating form of address, and one which is much affected by haughty menials, Bank of England clerks, ushers in courts of law, and other insolent and overbearing underlings. Providence, however, who seldom inflicts a bane without providing an antidote, has mercifully endowed the questioned one with the power of making the return inquiry, "What is what?" which, being unanswerable, has the effect of invariably shutting up, humbling, and morally squashing the miserable flunkey whose misconduct brings it down upon him.

Johnny, however, being depressed in mind, enfeebled in body, and entertaining altogether the poorest possible opinion of himself and his claims to an honourable reception, and, moreover, not being aware of the magnificent revenge which lay within his grasp, humbly replied that he should be glad to see Mrs. Pintle, if convenient.

"What might you wish with Mrs. Pintle?" asked the weak-eyed one.

"I am the late Mr. Pintle's confidential clerk; I wish to speak to her in that capacity."

"Oh! indeed, sir; walk in," said the weak-eyed

one, not feeling altogether sure whether Johnny had not succeeded in establishing his title to the visitors' bell after all, notwithstanding the depressing seediness of Johnny's appearance. He perhaps thought that this melancholy state of things was the natural result of the absorbing nature of the confidences which had been reposed in Johnny by Mr. Pintle. The Queen's Counsel, who dined now and then at the house, were seedy, so that after all that was no rule. So he showed Johnny into the library, and shortly returned with the information that Mrs. Pintle was in the drawing-room and would see him there. So Johnny walked up the softly-carpeted staircase, with much internal flutter, and much external mopping, and moreover, with much clearing of husky throat. He found Mrs. Pintle dressed in the deepest black, and reclining, in a spineless way, on a comfortable sofa.

Mrs. Pintle was a lady of fifty, or thereabouts. She was a lank, limp, lady, with pale straw-coloured hair, turning grey, in that underdone pie-crust looking way peculiar to straw-coloured hair in middle age. She was a perfect monument of black bombazine, crape, bugles, and jet, and if the depth of her sorrow could be fathomed in any way by reference to the funereal character of her appearance, she must have been a wife to be proud of. The memorial erected in Kensal Green to the late Mr. Pintle's memory, covered as it was with Scriptural references (which were, no doubt, anxiously overhauled by all visitors to that cheerful spot immediately on their reaching home), was an admirable conventional tombstone, as tombstones go, but it was entirely eclipsed in efficacy by Mrs. Pintle herself, who possessed peripatetic advantages which carried a mournful recollection of the deceased lawyer into the very bosom of her visiting acquaintance. The only question was as to the comparative duration of the two monuments. Every article of furniture which admitted of black drapery was smothered in it, and the envelopes and note-paper were black, with a small white parallelogram in the centre. As you gazed upon this melancholy state of things, you were almost tempted to wonder how it was that the pie-crust hair had not been placed in mourning also.

Johnny was immensely impressed by this dismal spectacle, and was much pleased at the contradiction it gave to the popular rumour that Mr. and Mrs. Pintle had not spent a particularly happy life together. He bowed with much reverence, an act which Mrs. Pintle acknowledged with a movement of the head, which bore the same relationship to an ordinary nod that the Old Hundredth does to an Irish jig.

"You were my dear husband's clerk, I believe," she remarked.

Johnny bowed.

"You can take a chair, if you have anything to say."

So Johnny sat down on the extreme edge of a very low *prie Dieu* chair, which was the only available seat immediately at hand, and twitched ner vously at his old hat; an operation which appeared likely to result in the immediate dissolution of that article of apparel. It is always an awkward thing, that hat. There are only three classes of visitors who are permitted to know what to do with it when they take it into a house which is not their own. The friend of the family, who comes to spend the evening, leaves it with the man in the hall, the ordinary visitor places it on an unoccupied chair, and the carpenter deposits it on the ground; but all others are required to hold it in their hands during an interview, and yet, if possible, to keep it out of sight. Johnny's was a self-assertive hat, which did not admit of easy concealment; so he fidgeted it about until it actually appeared to be taking a prominent part in the conversation.

"Now, then," said Mrs. Pintle, "what do you want? I suppose it's nothing about the will?"

"Nothing about the will, ma'am. I've not been in the way of hearing about it lately."

"Well, then, what in goodness's name do you want? Speak out, man, and have done with it."

Mrs. Pintle was one of that numerous class of mourners, whose grief takes the form of irritability. Besides, she had jumped to the conclusion that Johnny's visit referred to the missing document, and was disappointed.

"Ma'am, I've never done this before, but it's help I've come for. I've been Mr. Pintle's clerk, man and boy for five and forty year; and—and—now I'm in want, ma'am. I'm in absolute want. I've not come," said Johnny hurriedly, anxious that he should not be misunderstood, "I've not come, ma'am, to mention that, in the hopes that your kindness will immediately—will immediately"—(and he paused for a way of expressing it; and then added triumphantly) "will immediately put me right. God forbid. But if you would kindly put me or my wife (she's a young woman still) in the way of earning a livelihood—we don't care how humble it is, or how hard the work—we shall be deeply grateful."

"Is that all?" asked Mrs. Pintle, with a cold official air which did not promise well.

"I've no more to say, ma'am," added he, "except that I've been living in a sort of way, on charity mostly, for the last six weeks. I've tried to get work, and failed. I don't know how it is, but I've failed. I'm not young, ma'am, but I've got plenty of work left in me, if I could only find somebody who wants it."

"*That* is all, I presume?"

"That is all, ma'am."

"Then listen to me. My husband made a will, you know that?"

Poor Johnny knew it perfectly well. It had been the leading fact in his thoughts for weeks past, and there was no chance of his forgetting it. So he bowed.

"Very good. You know that my husband made a will. He placed it under your care. He gave it to you on the 22nd December. He died at midnight on the 24th. No will was to be found on the night of the 24th, and you have been unable or unwilling to produce it since. I don't know which, nor do I care. You can draw your own conclusions. Now you can go."

It burst upon Johnny all at once; a sort of suspicion appeared to attach itself to him that he knew more about the missing document than he cared to say. This was the solution of the difficulty he had experienced in getting employment from solicitors whom he had known, and with whom he had been friendly in better days.

"Mrs. Pintle," he exclaimed, "listen to me for one moment. Is it possible that I am suspected of having suppressed Mr. Pintle's will? It is a horrible thing to have to say in connection with one's self, but you seem to think that I know more than I have said. Good God! ma'am! why I am the greatest sufferer by its not being found. I am a legatee for £1,000. If it had turned up, my wife and I would have been independent by this time. As it is, my wife is dreadfully ill from want, and I have not a penny in my pocket—not a penny, not a penny!"

And old Johnny fairly gave way, and sobbed like a child on the crown of the self-assertive old hat.

"Will you oblige me by ringing that bell?" said Mrs. Pintle.

Johnny obeyed, and the weak-eyed one responded to the summons.

"Give this person some bread and cheese in the kitchen, and then show him out," said Mrs. Pintle.

Johnny got up, brushed the obtrusive hat the wrong way with a trembling hand, and silently turned about and followed the retainer downstairs. When he reached the foot, he made for the street door.

"Didn't you hear missus say you was to have some food?" asked the weak-eyed one.

But Johnny made no reply. He tugged at the street door with the view of getting into the street as quickly as possible. It was a complicated street door, with five or six small handles, and it was only to be opened by a combined tugging of two handles at once.

The weak-eyed one sauntered up to him, with his hands in his pockets, and watched Johnny's efforts with much complacency.

"Go on, old cock, try again. Never give it up. Go in and win." These and other remarks of an encouraging description, intended to spur Johnny on to fresh exertions, had the effect of irritating the poor old gentleman beyond all bounds.

"Damn you, open it, you dog, will you?" exclaimed Johnny with (for him) supernatural vehemence. And the weak-eyed one obeyed with an alacrity which one would scarcely have looked for in a man who a moment before was taking life in such a leisurely way.

Johnny tottered down the steps, shaking and trembling, and the weak-eyed one contemplated him from the door.

"Poor devil!" exclaimed he. "Mad as flints; quite as mad!"

And Johnny doddered on bravely, until he reached the corner of Guilford Street. He then began to feel that his strength was almost at an end; so he made an effort to turn round the corner, in order to get out of sight of the insolent flunkey, and, that accomplished, fell heavily to the ground.

CHAPTER III.

HOW JOHNNY POUNCE CAME BACK TO THE GOOD AGAIN.

"Cole, I shall want you at my quarters immediately after inspection."

"Very good, sir."

The scene of this remarkable dialogue was the Crimea before Sebastopol; the speakers were our old friend Captain Redfern of Her Majesty's —th Lancers, and Private John Coles of the same regiment, and regimental servant to Captain Redfern aforesaid.

Young John had proved to be too heavy and too tall a man for the friendly recruiting serjeant's corps, so he had been posted to a crack Lancer regiment then serving in the Crimea. In this regiment Captain Redfern held a commission, and as he went out in command of recruits, of whom young John was one, he was under the necessity of selecting one of them to act as a regimental servant during the voyage. His choice fell upon young John, who being extremely lazy and, moreover, utterly indifferent as to the future in store for him, accepted the situation.

Redfern and young John got on exceedingly well together. John's superior education made him extremely useful to his master in many ways, and as Redfern was a particularly open-handed man, and not very exacting as a master, he and John became, in a distant sort of way, attached to each other. Redfern spent much of his spare time in poring over deeds and other legal documents referring to the estate of which he had become possessed through Pintle's death; and as John was formerly in the habit of assisting his father in Mr. Pintle's office, he had picked up sufficient technical knowledge to make himself useful as an interpreter whenever Redfern (whose legal ideas were crude and elementary) found himself at a stand-still.

Captain Redfern's regiment was posted on the heights above Balaklava, but as he was attached temporarily to the staff of a general officer, his duties as aide-de-camp brought him continually on to the scene of action before Sebastopol. He had on this occasion been in attendance on his general at a divisional field-day in which his own regiment took part, and he availed himself of an opportunity of interchanging the few words already recorded, with his regimental servant before the parade was dismissed.

At the termination of the parade in question,

young John cleaned his horse and accoutrements, and then hurried off to Redfern's tent. He found his master in the act of sealing a goodly packet which appeared to contain a bundle of papers.

"Beg pardon, sir," said young John, saluting, "I believe you wanted me."

"Yes," said Redfern, "I want you particularly. Come in and sit down on that chest."

Young John obeyed.

"I believe," said Redfern, "you're a man to be trusted."

"I hope so, sir," said young John.

"I hope so, too. Well, I'm going to trust you. But in the first place I must enjoin you to utter secresy as to what I am about to say to you, until the time arrives when you may speak."

"You may trust me, sir; you may, indeed. I'll never breathe a word of it until you give me leave."

"Very good. Now listen. The attack is to be made to-night by the Second and Light Division. You will not be wanted, but I shall, for the general's brigade forms part of the attacking column. It will all be the orders in half an hour. I don't know whether or not you believe in predestination, nor do I care, but I do, and that is sufficient for my purpose. John Cole, I die to-night."

"I sincerely hope not, sir."

"Don't interrupt me. I die to-night; that, at least, is my firm impression. Now this is what I want you to do. I want you to take charge of this packet, which I now address to you. When I am dead you will open it, and act according to the instructions therein contained. If it should happen that I survive, I shall require it of you again, until I feel disposed to give it into your possession once more. Now may I trust you with this?"

"Indeed you may, sir, I'll take great care of it, but I sincerely trust it will not be in my keeping many hours."

"I hope not, my man, but we shall see. Now if after the attack I do not return to quarters, get leave to look after me: bring me in if you find me, and whatever you do, for God's sake don't leave my body in the open air longer than you can help. Now you can go. I shall want Bessie at half-past ten."

Young John saluted, and left the tent with the packet.

That night as Captain Redfern was carrying a message from one of the attacking columns to the reserve, he was struck by a rifle-ball, which entered his back and came out above his left arm. He died on the field within an hour of receiving the wound; and so his prophecy was verified.

Young John carried out his master's instructions faithfully. Shortly after receiving intelligence of Redfern's death he opened the packet, after having first satisfied the committee of officers that sat upon the dead man's effects, that it was duly addressed to him in Captain Redfern's handwriting. To his intense astonishment he found that it was directed to Mrs. Pintle. He was not aware of the relationship that existed between Mr. Pintle, and his late master, for although Captain Redfern was well known by repute to old Johnny long before Pintle's death, young John had never heard of his existence until he joined the ———th Lancers.

A memorandum, addressed to young John, accompanied the other enclosure. It was to the following effect:—

JOHN COLE,—When I am dead, take the enclosed packet to Mrs. Pintle, 74, Russell Square, London, as soon as you reach England. If there is any chance of your being killed before you leave the Crimea, entrust it to a comrade upon whom you can rely. If the attack to-night succeeds, it will probably not be necessary to do so. If you know no one else in whom you can place implicit confidence, give it to the Colonel.

I hereby make you, Private John Cole, C troop of Her Majesty's —th Lancers, the legatee of all my moveables in camp, with the exception of the gold watch I usually wear, which I leave to poor Annie Blake. Her address is High Street, Little Petherington. And I hereby appoint you the executor of this my last will and testament.

HERBERT REDFERN,
Capt. H.M. —th Lancers.

The Crimean war was at an end, and the troops

were on their way home again. Thinned and shattered as they were, they yet sufficed to afford evidence of the noble stuff they had left behind them, on Cathcart's Hill and in the Valley of the Shadow of Death. As they marched through great towns in their tattered uniform, with bear-skins and shakoes half shot away, their faces bronzed, and covered with ragged beard, and, above all, with their colours shot off almost to the pole, carried by dirty, ragged lads, who still somehow looked like gentlemen—lads who had already seen more misery and sickness in their young lives of twenty summers than the oldest spectator in the enthusiastic throng of civilians that gathered to welcome the old troops home again—as these sturdy warriors tramped through the English towns they had little expected to see again, women went into hysterics, and strong men, after shouting themselves hoarse with a kind of mad welcome that let itself go free to take what form it would, threw themselves down upon the grass, and there lay prone, and wept like women. For each man who saw a brother, or a friend, in those thinned and broken ranks, saw one whom he had hardly reckoned on ever seeing again; and he who counted no personal friends or relations among those rows of shattered warriors, saw thousands who had endeared themselves to him by their heroic pluck in battle, and, above even that, by their heroic and unmurmuring endurance of pain, privation, cold, disease, and hunger. And it was no disgrace to the men of peace that they did so weep, for even the staunchest heroes in that battle-thinned band—men who had laughed at the Russian shell, and laid wagers as to where it would fall; men of the "thin red line," who had fought at Balaklava and lit their cigars on the parapet of the Redan, marched that summer into Hyde Park, and as the Queen pinned the Cross of Valour over their sturdy hearts, choked themselves into tears that no physical anguish could have wrung from them.

Young John had risen in the service since the death of Redfern. He was now Troop Sergeant, and one of the smartest men in the squadron. His regiment was quartered at Hounslow on their return, and he was attached to the troop stationed at the old barracks at Kensington. His first care on reaching London was to find his father and mother. He had from time to time sent small sums of money to them, but he had never heard from them in reply, and it was with the apprehension of learning the details of some sad misfortune that he knocked at the old house in Great Queen Street.

The same drabby servant-girl opened the door, but she did not recognize young John in the strapping, set-up soldier, with the thick brown beard, who stood before her. She knew nothing of Johnny Pounce's whereabouts. He and Mrs. Pounce had left Great Queen Street eighteen months ago, owing much rent, and nobody in the house had heard of them since. She shouldn't wonder if they'd got into trouble. She had heard something about a will, and people said that they were no better than they ought to be. Oh, of course he could leave a message if he liked, but he might as well leave one for the Lord Mayor of London.

Young John turned away with an aching heart, for the full sense of his ingratitude in leaving them at the critical moment, burst upon him. He next called at Russell Square, with the object of placing Captain Redfern's packet into Mrs. Pintle's hands. But Mrs. Pintle had long since left the house in Russell Square, for it was a much larger establishment than she, in her reduced circumstances, could afford to keep up. The footman who opened the door told him that when Mrs. Pintle left she gave directions that all letters directed to her late residence should be forwarded to an address in Michael's Place, Brompton, but that was ever so many months ago, and she might not be there now. However, he had better go there and ascertain her present address if she had moved. So young John walked back to the Strand, and mounted a Brompton omnibus, which put him down at the address to which he had been directed.

He found Mrs. Pintle in drawing-room apartments in Michael's Place. He obtained admission to her without difficulty, for the weak-eyed flunkey had been dismissed with the rest of the household, as soon as Mrs. Pintle gave up all hope of finding her husband's will. She was reclining on a horsehair sofa of decidedly serious presence, and was still in mourning, but this time it was for her nephew.

She was surprised at seeing a brown-faced,

sturdy soldier enter the room, and her astonishment was not diminished when he announced himself as a soldier of the late Captain Redfern's regiment, for Captain Redfern and she had never been on particularly friendly terms, and since Mr. Pintle's death they had come to open war. The mourning that she wore was not by any means the result of emotion at that officer's death, but sprung from a species of natural taste for tombs, and everything that pertained thereunto.

"What is your business with me, soldier?" she asked.

"Beg pardon, ma'am; have I the honour of speaking to Mrs. Pintle?"

"You have."

"I'm the bearer of this parcel from the late Captain Redfern. He directed me to place it in your hands as soon as I returned to England. I only arrived four days ago, and I've availed myself of the first leave of absence I could get to bring it to you."

And young John touched his forehead, and wheeled about to depart.

"Stop," she said, "you must wait until I see what it is about."

And she attempted to open the parcel, but her hands trembled so that she could not unfasten the knots, so young John whipped out a pocket-knife, and solved the difficulty after the original Gordian receipt. The enclosure was contained in another wrapper, and upon this second wrapper being hastily torn asunder, there tumbled out of it a note addressed to Mrs. Pintle, together with the Will of the late Josiah Pintle!

Mrs. Pintle was one of those hard-faced ladies who have schooled their countenances to obey them implicitly. Mrs. Pintle's face was in a state of perfect discipline, and expressed no astonishment whatever. Not so, however, her voice.

"My God! my husband's will!"

Young John could scarcely believe the ears that conveyed Mrs. Pintle's exclamation to his brain, and felt much more disposed to trust to the eyes that told him that, judging from Mrs. Pintle's countenance, nothing extraordinary had happened. However, the same eyes subsequently contradicted themselves as he read the endorsement, "Will of Josiah Pintle, Esq."

"Mr. Pintle's will, ma'am!" he exclaimed; "I had no idea of that; he didn't tell me what it was. Why, my father is down in that for a thousand pounds!"

"And who is your father?"

"Pounce, ma'am; Johnny—I mean John Pounce, ma'am—the late Mr. Pintle's confidential clerk."

"Then your name is Pounce?"

"My real name is, ma'am; I enlisted, shortly after Mr. Pintle's death, as John Cole; but my real name is Pounce."

Mrs. Pintle, after satisfying herself that the will was genuine, proceeded to open the accompanying note. It was to the following effect:—

Before Sebastopol, 1856.

AMELIA PINTLE,

Long before this reaches you I shall be a dead man. We were never on friendly terms, and the words I am about to write will not tend to mend matters. Whether they do, or whether they do not, is a question that will not in any way disturb the skeleton that by that time will be bleaching in this infernal country.

You always considered me an extravagant and unconscientious scoundrel, and I give you credit for your discernment. I don't attempt to exculpate myself, because I do not care enough for you or for anybody in the world to make it worth my while to do so. As I have already stated, by the time this is opened I shall be dead beyond all possibility of doubt. I live only for life, and posthumous honour or dishonour is a matter upon which I am most completely indifferent. As evidence of my sincerity, I not only enclose Josiah Pintle's will, but I also give an account of the manner in which it came into my possession.

On the 24th of December, 1854, I dined with Mr. Pintle. On that occasion you were, you may remember, confined to your room by some sort of indisposition. After dinner, as Pintle and I sat over our wine, we talked over family matters, and, among others, of the disposition of his property after death. He told me that he had that evening brought his will to Russell Square with the express view of reading it over to me, in whom, you will remember, he reposed (contrary, I am bound to say, to your advice) much more confidence than I either desired or deserved.

He opened the document and began to read it to me as I sat with my back towards him, for he had turned round to get the full benefit of the light of the chandelier. He read for perhaps a couple of minutes, and then stopped: I concluded that he was considering the advisability of not reading to me the ensuing paragraph which might perhaps refer to a trifling legacy which he intended to bestow upon me. After a pause, I asked him why he did not go on, and, as he made no answer, I turned round to repeat my question. He was dead.

I alarmed the household; but, before they answered my summons, it occurred to me that, as I was his heir-at-law, and moreover deeply in debt, and further, as nobody but myself was aware of the fact that the will had been taken from the office, I might as well take possession of it and destroy it altogether. Accordingly I took possession of it, and, in due course, of the bulk of Mr. Pintle's property. On second thoughts I did not destroy the will, for, as I was under orders for the Crimea, I thought it possible that I might be killed, and, in the event of that melancholy occurrence, neither the will nor the property would be of any further use to me, whereas they might both prove of considerable value to yourself and the other legatees. So they are quite at your service.

HERBERT REDFERN,
Capt. H.M. —th Lancers.

THE KEY OF THE STRONG ROOM.

Mrs. Pintle folded the letter deliberately, restored it to its envelope, and placed the envelope in her pocket.

"I shall not want you, Pounce," she said. "If, as you say (and I see no reason to disbelieve it), your father is a legatee for a thousand pounds, he will, of course, receive it when the will is proved; that, however, will probably be, under the circumstances, a work of time. In the interim, as I have done your father the injustice of believing that he—that he did not act with perfect openness in the matter, I shall be happy to make him a small allowance. You had better send him to me."

"If I can discover him, ma'am, I will, but he's left his old lodgings, and no one knows where he has gone to!"

"Then find him. You had better advertise. Now you can go."

Young John left Mrs. Pintle's house with a heart almost as heavy as when he entered it, for there appeared but little chance of his finding old Johnny and his wife, and, moreover, he had made the discovery that his late master, for whose memory he entertained a sincere regard, was, in point of fact, an unmitigated scoundrel.

He had the rest of the afternoon before him, and he spent the early part of it in sending advertisements to the principal daily papers. It was four o'clock before this was satisfactorily accomplished, and then he took a steamboat from Blackfriars intending to go to Chelsea, and thence to Kensington.

But the boat did not go higher than Westminster bridge, so he landed there, and determined to take the omnibus at Charing Cross.

As he walked down Parliament Street, he had to pass the scene of his former labours, the Pauper Philosophy Office; which appeared, as far as he could see, to be getting on uncommonly well without him. There was the same old over-fed office-keeper at the door, there were the same two showy Caucasians waiting on the steps, and there were all the twelve Examiners looking out of the twelve windows, as of yore. There was the Lord President's carriage at the door, and there, no doubt, was the Lord President in the Secretary's room, learning a practical reply to the eminently practical question, which would be asked in the House that night, " Whether there was any truth in the statement that it was the practice of the Board for the Dissemination of Pauper Philosophy to educate and train young paupers to an extraordinary pitch of pauper perfection, at an enormous public expense, with the express view of qualifying such paupers to impart instruction in the rudiments of Pauper-Philosophy, and that accomplished, to take away from their sphere of duty such Pauper Philosophers as may seem to the Board to be peculiarly well qualified to train and educate other young paupers, and reward them with Assistant-Clerkships in the Office for the Dissemination of Pauper-Philosophy?"

As young John speculated on this possibility, it occurred to him that he would turn into the office and look up some of his old friends. He passed the Caucasians and the office-keeper unrecognized, and made his way up to the garret in which he had worked for the five years that preceded his dismissal.

It was just as he had left it, for promotion in the Pauper Philosophy Office was a work of many years. As he entered the room he was greeted with a stare of surprise, which was directed not so much at him (for he was unrecognized) as at the uniform he wore.

"Don't you know me, lads?" he said, "Pounce—John Pounce!"

"John Pounce!" exclaimed the five clerks. "Lord! you don't say so?"

And sufficiently hearty greetings ensued, for John had been a sort of favourite in his way.

Inquiries as to what events had occurred since he left the office followed; and one, more hearty than the rest, saw in young John's return a reason for standing much beer.

"Where's Shab?" asked the hearty clerk. "Send him here, somebody!"

And somebody went for Shab.

"Who's Shab?" said Johnny.

"Shab? Oh! you know—no, he's since your time. Oh! he's a rum un is Shab. He runs herrands, and fetches beer, and posts letters, and does hod jobs. Shab ain't his name—its affectionate for shabby genteel—so called 'cause he looks like a Member of Parliament down on his luck."

And the door opened, and Shab introduced his head.

"Want me, gentlemen? Anything I can do?"

"Here, Shab, old cock, a gallon of beer, and you so much as look at it and I'll knock your empty old head off. D'ye hear?"

This was a coarse speech, but it was not said unkindly. Shab was a general favourite, for he was always at hand when wanted, and never grumbled at his *honorarium*. He had seen better days, as the saying is, having originally been employed on odd jobs in the Pauper Philosophy Office as a law-stationer's clerk; but old age came upon him, and his hand trembled so that he became unfit for his work. So he became a hanger-on to the office in which he had temporarily served, and picked up occasional coppers as a kind of out-door message carrier.

"Why you look out of sorts; had your dinner, Shab?" asked a clerk.

"No, sir, no—not yet."

"Thought not; you look hungry. Here's a tanner for you—no, I haven't got it."

"Looks hungry," thought young John, "by Jove, he is hungry, too. Here, my man," added he, aloud, "here's a shilling for you, and in God's name get something to eat."

A clerk from another room burst into the office.

"What's this I hear about Jack Pounce come back again?" said the new comer. "Jack, old chap, doosid glad to see you. Why what are you doing in a uniform?"

The answer was interrupted by an extraordinary proceeding on the part of poor old Shab.

"Jack! Young John! O God!"

And poor old Johnny Pounce fell into his son's arms.

* * * * *

So old, so feeble, so broken, had cheery little Johnny Pounce become since he went to the Bad! His rusty old suit of clothes was the cast-off of a waiter, just as he himself was the cast-off of society. He was living in a miserable attic in Tothill Fields, and his once buxom little wife was in the fever ward of the Westminster Hospital.

There cannot be much need to tell how it all ended. How his son told him of the discovery of the missing will, how old Johnny and he went to Mrs. Pounce's bedside, and broke the news to her, gently at first, and then all at once with a sort of spasmodic rush; how Mrs. Pintle did her best (in a faded kind of way) to atone for the unjust suspicions which she had cast upon the old man; how the sick woman recovered her strength by slow degrees, until she was able to leave the Hospital for the old rooms in Great Queen Street; how the will was proved beyond dispute, after a lapse of six months or so; how One Thousand Pounds were paid to old Johnny, without deduction, by Mrs. Pintle, and how a handsome annuity was purchased for him with the money; how young John was bought out of the service, and enshrined in a high desk in the office of Pintle and Sims' successors, having been articled to the new firm by Mrs. Pintle herself, who further undertook to make him an allowance until he was admitted—are matters that would take many pages to tell in detail, and matters, moreover, which the reader will probably feel inclined to take for granted.

And so it was that Johnny Pounce, having gone to the Bad, and having spent a considerable time at the Bad when he got there, eventually came back to the Good again.

THE KEY OF THE NURSERY CUPBOARD.

THE KEY OF THE NURSERY CUPBOARD.

If you open the nursery cupboard you will see——

But before I tell you what you will see, I think perhaps I ought to tell you the whole story.

At the time when the old *noblesse* fled terrified before the first fierce upheaval of that overwhelming volcano, the French Revolution, a Monsieur Delaval made his appearance in the little town of Bincester, in Essex, and put a modest advertisement into the local paper that he was desirous of giving lessons in French, Italian, and drawing. He found pupils and employment at the various schools in the town before long, but not before his scrupulously neat dress showed signs of age and long wear. It was only from this evidence, which he could not conceal, that even Mrs. Martin, the widow, with whom he lodged, was able to see how straitened the poor gentleman's circumstances were. Even when she knew it she found it quite impossible to offer him any show of assistance, for Monsieur Delaval was not a person to take charity with a good grace.

Honest Mrs. Martin was sorely touched to see his little girl—" the image of my Mary," Mrs. Martin would say—for the child was often very, very hungry, and looked thin and ill. But the widow received a lesson from Monsieur the teacher, for which she did not pay, but which she never forgot. She had asked the child, as it was sitting out in the garden under the lilacs, singing some quaint old French song, to come in and have a little of her tart at dinner-time. The poor little thing at first refused, though its eyes said "Yes." It was plain that it acted under orders. But presently, child-like, it found the temptation too strong, and Monsieur passing the door saw it in the midst of its enjoyment of such jam and such puff-paste as only Mrs. Martin knew how to make. A few short, sharp words in French sent the little one upstairs in tears, and Monsieur, turning to Mrs. Martin, said that he "did not permit Mademoiselle Delaval to accept invitations from persons, and without consulting him. If she required refreshments, she would find them in her own apartments." And he said this, as Mrs. Martin described afterwards, "as proud as a nobleman!"

Where Mrs. Martin had formed her idea of the pride of a nobleman I cannot tell, for there was nothing higher than a baronet within miles of Bincester, and she knew very little of him even. But if she evolved the notion out of her inner consciousness, she was more successful than many cleverer people have been in so doing. Monsieur Delaval was as proud as a nobleman because he *was* a nobleman, and one, too, with more than the ordinary pride of his rank. The Counts de Lavalle from time immemorial had been among the haughtiest of the haughty French aristocracy. It was a tradition in the family that when Charlemagne passed through the province of the first count of the name, that noble received him hat on head, and on terms of the most perfect equality. "The rest of the world," said he, "belongs to you, sire, but the Count de Lavalle is Emperor here!" His descendants had been worthy of the *grand seigneur*, and "as proud as a de Lavalle" passed into a proverb.

When the Revolution broke out, the nobles of the count's neighbourhood enrolled themselves and their retainers, and took up arms for the defence of their property against the mob, and for a time were successful. But the count was not among them. It is true he had mustered his vassals and armed them, but when he found that the command was to be given to Monsieur Le Baron de Vieuxmesnil, he retired in dudgeon. Now, the baron was a general, a soldier by profession, and the nobles, who would have admitted the hereditary claims of the count if the country only had required defence, were wisely appreciative of experience and ability, when the question was one of their own personal safety. So the Count de Lavalle retired to his chateau in disgust. "He had troubled himself," he said, "to assemble a force for the protection of these others, and they disregarded the honour. Let them guard themselves! For his part he had no fear for himself. The rabble would not dare to come near him, and in the surrounding country the lower orders had too intimate a knowledge of and too great a regard for the traditions of the de Lavalles!"

The traditions of the de Lavalles best known to the surrounding peasantry were traditions of ancient wrong and tyranny, and injustice. The result was, that one night the château de Lavalle was the centre of a fierce and furious horde, that danced round singing its fierce song of vengeance as the red flames shot up their lithe tongues to the frightened sky, and a pillar of fire and blood-red smoke rose above the hideous orgie. From that conflagration and the *cordon* of fiendish savages, not a soul belonging to the de Lavalle household escaped save the count himself. He came forth bearing his child on his left arm, and carrying his drawn sword in his right hand. Whether it was fear of that glittering skilful blade, or some strange impulse of pity and remorse at the sight of the poor child, which exerted a charm over the mob, it is impossible to say, but it is certain that the line opened to allow the count to pass unharmed with his precious burden. That burden, by the way, was more precious than the mob suspected. The child carried enfolded in her arms, as she nestled terrified on her father's shoulder, a little casket containing the heirlooms of the de Lavalles. The family had not been a wealthy one of late—indeed cared less for riches than birth at any time—but some antique jewels of great value had been treasured with great reverence, one of them, known as "the de Lavalle topaz," being regarded especially with almost superstitious veneration. The count had been a widower some three years or so. He had therefore preserved, in preserving his child and the jewels, at once the hopes and the traditions of his family—its future and its past.

What induced him on reaching England to adopt Bincester as his place of abode is not clear. Why he adopted teaching as a professor is less difficult to discover. It was the only means of earning a living that was possible for him. He was fitted for nothing else, as was the case with very many of the French refugees who found shelter in England about this time.

Although not personally popular among his pupils, Monsieur Delaval—for the count changed his name as well as dropped his title—soon became well known in Bincester and all round about as a most successful teacher. His manner was cold, even stern, but he spoke always to the point, and so clearly and decidedly, that he seldom failed to impress his words on the recollection of his hearers. And he never endangered his authority by allowing familiarity, or anything remotely approaching it, to grow up between himself and those he taught.

His one fault was a hasty temper, but he kept it in great subjection. Stupidity of the most hopelessly crass description could not wear out his patience; inattention and idleness he was decided with, but they never elicited any token of anger from him. But an apparent slight, the least rudeness or forgetfulness of the respect due to him, would make his cheek livid and wake a dangerous fire in his eye. In very extreme cases he had been roused to the expression of his feelings in words;—though passionate and strong, these words never approached vulgar abuse or sank into shrewish invective. But it was universally agreed that it was a perilous work to quarrel with Monsieur Delaval. Even those non-respecters of persons, the school boys, knew that, and made quite sure that he was not within hearing when they said "Old Delaval" and "Mossoo Mopstick." That they should not have had a nickname for him it would be too much to expect of human nature. They despised everything French like intelligent young Britons, as they were, but they could not help feeling awe for him, partly on account of a story well known to all the boys of Bincester.

There was at one of the schools in the town, the son of a poor nobleman who had won for himself a distinguished position in the Lower House, and held a subordinate place in the Ministry. The lad had been sent to get his education cheaply at Bincester. Now boys, we know, are ardent politicians—the more ardent because, as a rule, they know nothing about politics—and a classmate of this lad's, whose father was of opposition politics, had taunted him with a rumour which he had picked up, Heaven knows how. The taunt was a little too sharp for the boy, and it chanced that Delaval came upon him as he was wiping away the tears.

"Crying?" said he, with a half sneer. "In my country the son of a nobleman does not know what tears are."

"He called my father names, and said he sold himself to Government," sobbed the lad.

"He did!" said the Frenchman sharply, "and you—what did you do to him?"

"What could I do, sir?"

"You should have k—— but I forget! It is only the French language that I have to teach you," was the answer, and Monsieur Delaval went on his way, but the boy said afterwards, "I'm sure he was going to say 'killed'—and oh, didn't he grind his teeth and turn white!"

Bincester, as has been already hinted, was not overrun with people of rank, but its inhabitants were a decent, obliging, and well-disposed set of people, as little morally injured by trade as is possible. They were not always cudgelling their brains to get a profit out of you, and did not look upon all relations of life as business relations of which a debtor and creditor account was to be kept mentally. They were very willing to make a friend of the French master, and for the first few years of his sojourn in the town, plied him with plentiful invitations for himself, and still more numerous ones for his daughter. But these were all declined, very politely, it is true, but in a manner which mingled a tone of surprise with a very decided hint that neither he nor Mademoiselle Delaval had any desire to make acquaintances in Bincester.

The good people of that town were not disposed to make themselves miserable at his refusal, though they were perhaps a little sorry that they could not make friends with his daughter, who had grown up into a very pretty girl, and was so graceful, and unassuming, and good, that it is no wonder she was sought after.

Valerie Delaval herself probably was as much inclined to make friends as the Bincester people, but her father would not permit it. She was taught to hold aloof, and decline all advances to acquaintance :—just as in her childhood, when Mrs. Martin offered her some dainty, she used to say her lesson, "No, thank you, I'm not hungry—I couldn't eat it." But just as in those days the big grey eyes used to look wistfully at the tempting bit, so now they showed how she hungered for friendship and the companionship of those of her own age and sex. Despite her father's lectures, she found it quite impossible to treat Mrs. Martin as distantly as he wished her to do. "Mademoiselle de Lavalle forgets herself when she associates with the widow of a shop-keeper!" he would say. So poor Valerie was very solitary, and spent her young days wearily. At last she found a pet, something on which to bestow her affection. It was not a very lovely object, but she became very fond of it. It was a poor cur—a lost and half-starved creature, which had followed her to the door, and pleaded so piteously for food and shelter, that she had taken it in and adopted it. Her father was far from delighted at the acquisition. "*Morbleu*, if it had been an Italian greyhound or a well-bred dog of any description! But this mongrel! *Ma chère* Valerie, I fear you have not the tastes of a de Lavalle!"

Certainly poor Chicine was no beauty. Her coat was long and wiry, and stuck about stubbornly in unexpected elf-locks. She had lost an ear, and one eye was partially blind, and she had, oh, such a stump—such a very abridged stump of a tail. It seemed as if the Fates, otherwise exceedingly hard upon her, had mercifully provided against any possibility of her having a tin kettle tied to it. Still, though outwardly unprepossessing, Chichine was remarkably beautiful, morally. Her attachment to Valerie was a thing touching to witness. But it did not propitiate Monsieur Delaval. "*Peste!*" he said, "for what are these lower animals made? It is the least thing that they should be devoted servants of man." He said it in a manner which seemed to imply that since the dog was intended to be devoted to the human race, it was very small credit indeed that it should be so to one of the de Lavalle family. He perhaps had something the same sort of idea about a canine traditional regard for that name that he had about the traditional loyalty of the lower orders to it, just before they burned his château over his head. However he suffered Valerie to keep the poor cur, though he made her feel at times that it was retained under protest.

When Valerie reached the age of twenty-one, her father made a modest fête on her birthday. They had a tasteful little dessert after dinner, and a bottle of French wine, of which a glass was sent down to Mrs. Martin, with directions to drink the health of Mademoiselle Delaval. The good woman repeated the toast, but didn't drink the wine, which she pronounced sour as vinegar.

On this day the schoolmaster was laid aside, and the Count de Lavalle presided at the frugal table. And when he had drunk the toast with great grace and dignity, and Valerie had jumped up and flung her arms round his neck and kissed him, he brought out all that was left him of the de Lavalle estates, —the casket of jewels and his sword. He made a long and impressive speech to Valerie—bidding her remember that she was the last of the noble line, and pointing out to her the duties and responsibilities that devolved upon her. Then he placed the casket in her hand, and making a tender allusion to the time when she bore those heirlooms in safety from the burning château, told her the jewels were hers henceforth.

"There is, my child, another priceless jewel which you have in your keeping—the honour of the de Lavalles. Guard it well, for there must be a restoration of our rights some day. Until then, you have the jewels—and I the sword," and Monsieur le Comte de Lavalle unwound the flannel bandages in which his sword was carefully swathed, solemnly imprinted a kiss on the glittering blade, and lifted it silently towards heaven.

The next day the schoolmaster was assumed

once more, and the nobleman laid by with the jewels and the sword.

Not long after this, a circumstance occurred which was fated to influence the history of the Delavals. Valerie, with her faithful Chichine, was walking in the woods not far from Bincester, when the poor dog, straying into a plantation by the roadside, was caught in a gin. Valerie was in terrible distress and anguish, and did all she could to release her pet, but in vain. Chichine having exhausted all means of extricating herself, was lying on her side panting and looking askance at her mistress, who was endeavouring to undo the cruel wire.

"Let me assist you," said a man's voice. Valerie looked up, and saw a tall handsome-looking young man standing beside her. She blushed and felt shy,—she had had little experience of the society of strangers, but the occasion was too pressing to admit of hesitation, so she accepted the offer gratefully. The gentleman knelt beside her, and in a few moments had extricated Chichine from the snare. The dog, instead of recognizing the services thus rendered, made use of its freedom to retire behind its mistress and snarl angrily at its liberator.

"Fie, Chichine! is that the way in which you express your thanks? Let me apologize, Monsieur, for Chichine's want of manners. I am indeed indebted to you."

"That more than repays the little act. I can consent to do without Chichine's acknowledgments. I must speak to the keeper and tell him not to set his traps so close to the road—that is, if you are often in the habit of walking this way."

He said this carelessly, but it was plain that he expected an answer.

"Oh, Chichine and I come here very often."

"I am glad to hear it, for when I am at home the woods are a favourite haunt of mine, and I may perhaps have the pleasure of seeing you again and giving Chichine an opportunity of saying 'Thank you,' when her temper has recovered its serenity, which the trap has very naturally disturbed."

He was sauntering along by her side; his manner was very pleasant and kind, and Valerie confessed to herself he was handsome, and felt he was a gentleman. He on his side was immensely taken with Valerie, who was now a woman in appearance, with a fine figure and a beautiful face, all the more beautiful for the absence of conscious beauty.

So they wandered on, and the shyness of Valerie wore off, and the gentleman was most agreeable and chatty, and treated her with such politeness and respect that she felt quite at her ease. By and by, when they came to the high road to Bincester, they separated. As they were parting, he said, as if a thought suddenly struck him, "I ought to have introduced myself long before this. My name is Balfern; you probably know my father, Admiral Balfern, by name."

Valerie had frequently heard of the Admiral in Bincester, where he was a very great personage, being, in fact, the one baronet spoken of at the beginning of this story as the "nobleman" of the neighbourhood.

Although young Balfern made no request to learn her name, Valerie felt that she ought to tell him, in her turn, who she was.

"I am Valerie Delaval," she said, shyly; "my father is a teacher of languages in Bincester."

"Oh! I have heard of Monsieur Delaval often; his reputation as an able master is wide-spread; I hope we shall be acquainted. Good bye, Mademoiselle Delaval; I trust this will not be our last meeting."

He did not seem quite sure whether she would shake hands with him; but she did, in all frankness. You see she had had no opportunity of learning the *convenances*, and she followed the dictates of her heart, which was warm, and generous, and trustful.

"Good bye, Chichine!" But Chichine only growled, and showed her few remaining teeth.

And so the pair separated.

Valerie did not revisit the woods for several days. She was afraid that Reginald Balfern would think her over-bold; but it must be confessed she felt a strong inclination for a walk in that direction —an inclination which, at last, she found it impossible to overcome. Accordingly, one day, she and Chichine found themselves once again in Admiral Balfern's plantation. They had not walked far before Chichine sprang forward, barking fiercely, and made a rush towards a gate on which Reginald

Balfern proved to be sitting, when Valerie came up.

"You ungrateful Chichine," said Valerie. "Oh, Monsieur Balfern, what an ungrateful creature; isn't she?" and she shook hands with him.

"I thought you had forsaken the woods; I have not seen you since the day of Chichine's mishap; have you been here?"

"No; I have hardly been out of doors since."

"Ah, you should make the most of this weather; it will not last long; you see the leaves are turning already; look, they have even begun to fall. We shall have fogs and damps soon, when Balfern woods will not be the best place for a promenade."

He fell into his old place by her side, and they strolled along, talking pleasantly. They were quite like old friends now, and by the end of the walk there began to creep into existence another feeling than friendship.

Before the threatened fogs and damps came, and while yet the red, and russet, and gold glories were lingering on the woods, these two young people had met again and again, and their love was no secret between them, though it had never been confessed. That love had become Valerie's life now. All the treasured passion of her nature centred in Reginald Balfern; her solitary life had not allowed her affection to run to waste; it was hoarded up for this time and this man. She worshipped him; and so, when the moment came, and he asked her to give him her heart, she could only tell him that it was his already, and let her head sink on his shoulder, while, through the mist of happy tears, all golden dreams of bliss, and peace, and content, floated before her eyes.

It had not been with any intention of concealment originally that Valerie had not told her father of her acquaintance with young Balfern. She did not tell him of the first meeting, because she fancied he might become alarmed at her solitary walks, and forbid them, and because she did not wish to cause him anxiety.

By and by, when her heart became the shrine of a deep and earnest love, the subject was too sacred to be spoken of. And now when the love was confessed, and she and Reginald had plighted faith, she learned that there was a reason for continuing her silence. The Admiral, Sir Matthew Balfern, was a specimen of the old school of naval officers—a man full of strong prejudices, quick tempered, obstinate, domineering. He ruled his household as if it had been a man-of-war, and his language and bearing were those of the quarter-deck. And among his strongest and most enduring prejudices was a hatred of France and Frenchmen.

Reginald Balfern, his son, had been brought up in slavish fear and obedience, as might be expected. He did not know what it was to have a wish or will of his own in opposition to his father, until he met Valerie, when love as usual broke down all barriers. But Reginald still stood in terrible awe of the Admiral, and dreaded, above all things that he should learn how his son was paying attention to a

Frenchman's daughter. Above and beyond this Reginald was selfish—irredeemably selfish, and if he feared to disobey his father by force of his education in the dread of his wrath, he also was anxious not to suffer the consequences of that disobedience, for the old man's first threat on every occasion was to "cut him off with a shilling, and leave him a beggar!" There was, under these circumstances, a very powerful reason for his trying to conceal his attachment for Valerie. His father had been married a second time, and to a widow with two grown-up daughters, and there was no love lost between him and his step-mother, who was very anxious to contrive the usurpation of his place in his father's affections by her daughters. The old gentleman, however, had his family pride, and there was no fear of Reginald's being superseded, so long as he did nothing to bring himself into disgrace.

He laid all this before Valerie, and begged her to keep their engagement a secret, which she readily consented to do. He was hers; that was enough. She was content to wait patiently for years, calm in the consciousness of his love. The knowledge of that seemed the perfection of happiness, and she needed nothing more.

Meantime Chichine, having at length been induced to overcome her dislike to Reginald, had rushed into the other extreme, and was as extravagantly fond of him. Unluckily for her, she had not the sense to reserve the demonstrations of her affection for the proper occasion, and accordingly one day, to Reginald's horror, when he had driven into Bincester with his step-mother for some shopping, he found Chichine yelping and jumping about his legs with every token of delight and friendship. The next time he met Valerie he told her of this unfortunate indiscretion of the dog's.

"You must get rid of that dog, Valie darling. Lady B. is as keen as a needle, and if she had seen Chichine with its owner would have made dangerous conjectures. Chichine must go."

Valerie's eyes filled with tears at the thought, and she pleaded for her favourite, to whom, she reminded Reginald, they owed their acquaintance. But Reginald's safety was concerned, and therefore Reginald had no mercy. Valerie was ready to sacrifice anything for him, so devoted and blind was her love. So poor Chichine was handed over to Mrs. Martin, with orders that she should be given to some one who would be kind to her. And Valerie being questioned as to the reason of her parting with her pet, said that it was because "papa did not like dogs, and Chichine annoyed him much, though he would not say so."

But Chichine was not so easily to be got rid of. She returned from her new home so often, that at last it became necessary to try and send her away to some distance. So she was given to a bargeman who was going up the canal, with orders to keep her tied up for two or three days. But even this was not successful. Within a week after her departure, Chichine was back again, half starved

and travel-stained, and ready to drop with fatigue.
Valerie was so touched by this fidelity, that she
could not find heart to send the dog away again,
and when next she met Reginald, tried to obtain
a reversal of the sentence of banishment. She
learned, however, that on her way home this last
time, Chichine had passed Balfern House, had recognized Reginald at a window, which opened on the
lawn, and had rushed in, and covered him with
muddy caresses, to the great astonishment of the
family, who were at breakfast. He had been obliged
to order the servants to drive her away with whips,
to her utter bewilderment. This had sealed her fate.
Reginald told Valerie that a friend and brother
officer of his was about to sail in a few days, and
would take Chichine on board, and thus for ever
bear her beyond reach of mischief. Valerie sorrowfully consented, and took a farewell of her old
favourite, and Reginald carried Chichine off with
him, and going to the river after he parted from
Valerie, tied a stone round the poor dog's neck and
deliberately drowned it. A few days after, Valerie,
walking on the banks of the Bin, saw the bloated
but still recognizable corpse of poor Chichine aground
in a creek. It was a warning, but a vain one. She
did not for a moment suspect Reginald.

And thus time glided on, and Reginald and
Valerie met frequently, and forgot, in the idle purposeless dreaming of love, the stern necessities of
real life, until one day the former learnt from a
letter, written by a friend in London, that he would

soon be recalled to his ship, which was to be ordered to join the fleet.

Then the two young people were obliged to look this actual world in the face. And each looked at it from a different point of view. Valerie was heartbroken at the thought of Reginald's leaving her— and leaving her to face the dangers of war. But beyond that she thought of nothing. Reginald, on the other hand, felt anxiety chiefly because he feared that in his absence some other might step in and carry off Valerie; and yet he dreaded to discover their love to his father. The only possible way by which he could secure Valerie, and yet not endanger his position with his father, was a secret marriage. To this he hardly dared to hope that Valerie would consent. He formed his opinion partly, it is true, from his knowledge of Valerie's character, which was too noble and frank to deal readily in concealment and evasion; but we know that love, though it often enhances our virtues, can, when needful, make us consent to meannesses we should not dream of in our sober senses. Reginald's chief reason, however, for supposing that Valerie would refuse to marry him secretly was the consciousness that he himself, in a like case, would hesitate before making such a bad bargain. He judged of her by himself, and he was wrong. She loved him far too well not to condescend to the measure he proposed, and she never thought of herself. For her part, she could have trusted him, and hoped and waited on; but as he wished to make her his wife, she was ready. She must be his wife; she could be no other's; what did it matter whether it was now or in a few years, if it was publicly known, or a secret like their love?

The de Lavalles belonged to the old Huguenot nobility, so there was no difficulty in the question of religion, and Reginald speedily found means of making Valerie his bride under circumstances of the utmost secrecy.

His departure was unexpectedly delayed longer than he anticipated, his vessel having been detained to form part of a convoy. Before he left England his wife confided to him the tender news which should make a young husband's heart so full of joy, and pride, and happy solicitude. But Reginald was only rendered anxious and terrified. He once again bound Valerie by the most solemn obligations not to reveal their marriage to any one under any circumstances. It was impossible that he did not see what misery unspeakable this must entail upon her, but it was not in his nature to consider how great were the sacrifices he exacted, provided only that he was ensured against discomfort or loss.

It was rather to prepare against any extremity which might endanger his secret than with a desire for her well-being and peace of mind that he gave Valerie the address of his old nurse, who was a pensioner of the family, living down by the sea-coast in her native village. In any difficulty he told Valerie to write to her.

In a few days he had sailed.

Poor Valerie! So young, so inexperienced, so

innocent! She little knew the terrible consequences of her promise. It was only one sweet hope that she saw of the future—the dark terrible side was disregarded. But the day of anguish, and trial, and tribulation came at last.

It is impossible to describe the horror and anger of Monsieur Delaval when he discovered, as he believed, the shame which had fallen on his house!

"Wretched girl! how long is it since I told you that the honour of the house of de Lavalle was in your keeping?"

Poor Valerie, who had sunk into a chair at the first outburst of the storm, could only rock to and fro with a low moaning. She had of late begun to dread this, but she never thoroughly realized it until it came.

"What have I done," said the old man fiercely, "that this dishonour falls upon me in my old age— that my grey hairs are disgraced? *Mon Dieu*, what have I done to deserve this?"

As he glanced upwards, defiantly almost, his eye caught the sword which hung over the mantelpiece. He snatched it down and tore off the covering.

"True! You are my friend. I know my duty." Then turning to Valerie, he said, in a harsh, hoarse whisper, "His name!"

But she only stretched out one hand deprecatingly, and sobbed as though her heart were breaking.

"Miserable creature, is it not enough that you have brought shame upon me?"

"No, no, I have not, father," was all she could find strength to utter.

"Liar, as well dishonoured! You have lost for ever the good name of the de Lavalles which was entrusted to your keeping. Tell me his accursed name, that I may wash out this stain in his blood."

"No, no! It cannot—it must not be. I am innocent."

"You persist in your falsehood. You are surely no de Lavalle—a de Lavalle never lies. But his name! His name! By Heaven I *will* have his name!"

He caught her by the wrist with his left hand and shook her fiercely.

"His name—his name!"

"Never!" she gasped. The brutality had roused the spirit of the daughter. She faced him now as bold as himself. He paused for a moment—looked at her with a gaze of concentrated rage and hate, and then flung her from him.

"*Mon Dieu!* lost—lost to everything. Nameless—shameless—abandoned; go—leave me. Out of my sight—let me never see you again. And you," he looked at his sword, "once guardian of the honour of my race, your task is done! I am an old man, and must die soon, and the honour of the de Lavalles is departed. Your mission is at an end—there is no more need of you. My heart is broken. Break you, too, spotless blade, break!"

He placed the sword across his knee—a snap, a tinkling clash—and he flung the broken weapon from him, sank into a chair, and burst into an agony of tears.

Then all Valerie's anger melted away, and she stole up and tried to soothe him. But at the first touch of her hand he shrank back and sprang to his feet.

"Touch me not! Your touch is defilement—disgraced, dishonoured, shameless wanton! Go, I say. Leave this roof. You are no child of mine—go!"

He waved her off furiously—his voice choked—he staggered a moment, and then fell heavily to the ground in a fit.

Valerie rang the bell in terror, and sent Mrs. Martin for a doctor. Monsieur Delaval was placed on his bed, and before long began to recover, but only to sink into a state of feverish, delirious weakness. Even through the shadow of madness and the mists of half-insensibility he kept crying to them to take Valerie out of his sight. She left the room at last, for the doctor said his patient would be no better while she stayed there. Then she seated herself on the threshold outside the bedroom door, and listening, weeping bitterly, but in silence. She could hear him still moaning, "Thrust her from my roof. Shamed, shamed." And he continued complaining thus until the opiate which the doctor had administered began to take effect, and he fell into an uneasy slumber.

The doctor coming out of the room at last, almost fell over Valerie, who, exhausted by her emotion and the terrible anxiety of the scene she had gone through, had sunk against the door-post almost swooning. She asked the doctor faintly if her father was better—out of danger.

"Yes, I trust, madam," said he, very stiffly—he was a harsh man, and very cold—"but I cannot answer for his life unless my orders are obeyed. Your presence will endanger his recovery. You must not go near him," and he went away without even wishing her good morning. Mrs. Martin, too, was very frigid, and would hardly speak to her. It almost broke poor Valerie's heart to find every one shrinking from her.

What was she to do? This was no longer a home for her—she must find shelter elsewhere. So she packed up her few clothes and trinkets, and determined to go to her husband's old nurse.

For a long time she was uncertain what she should do about the jewel-casket. It was hers, she felt, and she had done nothing to forfeit it. By and by, when her husband came home and claimed her openly as his wife, she could return to her father and say, "I have kept all the jewels of the de Lavalles, and that priceless jewel—our honour. Take me back to your arms!" Yes, she would retain the casket. If her father was angry at her doing so for a while, he would know all before long.

She stole into his room to take one last look at

him before she went away. He was sleeping calmly now. She crept to the bedside, kissed his hand, and bathed it with tears. As she did so, she heard him murmur, " Lost! lost! Take her out of my sight!" Even in his dreams this terrible mistake was haunting him. It was like a stab to her poor heart, and she hurried from the room.

"Reginald—dear Reginald—husband!—what am I not suffering for your sake!"

It had, indeed, been a painful struggle. But Valerie was determined to keep her solemn promise to her husband. She knew that if she told her father, and tried ever so hard to convince him of the necessity of keeping the marriage a secret he would refuse to do so. He would not understand how any one could feel dishonoured by an alliance with the de Lavalles, and he would not consider that her husband's interests were at all comparable with the necessity for guarding the name of de Lavalle from even the shadow of suspicion.

So with her little box she took her departure for the village where her husband's nurse resided. It was a small fishing place, about thirty miles from Bincester to the north, and was to be reached without great difficulty. She had to take a fly from Bincester to Sibley cross-roads, where she took the coach that carried her within four miles of the seaside village, which was called Halborough. It was a poor little village, dependent for support on the sprat fishery. It was situated on a belt of marsh that extended for miles along the coast, and behind it stretched away leagues of rich corn land, protected from the floods which over-ran the marshes by an embankment. Halborough itself stood on a little knoll which sometimes in severe winters, when the waters were out, became an island.

It was a dreary, desolate place at the best of times, but it was at its dreariest and darkest pitch of desolation when Valerie reached it. Winter was far advanced, and the marshes were immense lakes of leaden-coloured water, taking their colour from the leaden sky whence the rain was descending in lashing torrents. Scarcely seen through the drift, a dark sea, edged with cruel white foam that looked like monstrous fangs devouring the coast, filled up the background of a straggling village of poverty-stricken houses, most of them mere hovels. To be sure Valerie entered the place on the worst side. At the further end there was a handful of decent cottages and shops—for it was frequented by a few visitors in the summer, and had humble pretensions to being a watering-place. It was just large enough to be inhospitable, and just small enough to be scandalous. There were too many inhabitants to form the little family group which so many little hamlets present, and there were too few for them not to find everybody else's business more interesting than their own.

Mrs. Booth's house was on the borders of the genteel quarter, but it was but a humble, shabby-genteel sort of place. It was a shop of the "all sorts" kind, displaying in its window—which was not a shop window, but an ordinary one—bits of work, small articles of drapery, toys and sweets, and some modest stationery. The old woman did not drive a brisk trade, but she was not dependent on her shop, having a sufficient living in the pension she received from the old admiral.

A grim woman was Mrs. Booth, who had been the tyrant of nurseries, and had never softened to any child but Reginald. When the poor children of Halborough came to expend their mites in her shop no kindly impulse ever induced her to tilt the scale in their favour, by adding one "sweet drop" beyond the exact weight—though, as we know, she only kept the shop as an employment not as a livelihood.

She gave Valerie no very warm reception. Reginald had told her of his marriage with the daughter of a French teacher, and had asked her to give his wife what advice and assistance she could when the time of trouble came, as come it must, he knew very well. Mrs. Booth at once concluded that he had been entrapped into a marriage by some designing girl, and took an immediate dislike to Valerie without having seen her. But she of course determined to do all that Reginald asked her to do. She would have died for him—have suffered any pain or discomfort to save him from trouble. It is curious to observe how often selfish people get this sort of devotion, and from how many people—

women more especially. There was one thing which the old woman had made up her mind to do—to persuade Valerie, no matter by what means, to forego her claim to be Reginald's wife. It was a hard savage design from one woman to another, an utter forgetfulness of all sympathy for her sex; but you remember that Mrs. Booth had only one tender place in her heart—her affection for the boy she had nursed.

She gave up to Valerie the room over the shop. It was a dark, smoky chamber, but it was the best in the house, and it was better furnished than any of the others. When Mrs. Booth left the family to come here, Reginald's mother, who was a good, sweet woman—she might have changed her son's nature had she lived longer—gave her all the furniture of the nursery, with which the old woman had filled up this room. Over the mantelpiece hung an old picture of a child's head; not Reginald's portrait, but a portrait of a little girl, one of the Balfern family, in which the nurse had said she saw a strong likeness to the boy, and which she had begged of her mistress. It was not a valuable picture, and no one knew whom it represented, but if it had been twice as important, Lady Balfern could not have refused it to her boy's faithful and devoted nurse.

Before Valerie had been with her long, Mrs. Booth perceived that she was in error as to her having entrapped Reginald. Her love for him was too real and unaffected. But the old nurse was nevertheless still determined if possible to separate her from him. He must marry some one worthy of him, not the child of a poor schoolmaster.

She was not astonished to find that Valerie was ardently attached to Reginald. That seemed to her only natural. He was a sultan in her eyes, who had only to throw his handkerchief to make a woman his slave for life. It was through this devotion that she first tried to work out her project. She pointed out to Valerie that she was ruining the man she loved. His place was high up in the world, but she was dragging him down.

"If you are as fond of him as you say, you must see that. His whole career is spoilt by your marriage, and he might have aimed so high. If I were placed as you are, I would never ask for recognition."

"Good Heavens, woman, what are you counselling?"

"For the happiness of the man you profess to be ready to die for. This is not as much as dying. You will still be his wife in reality, whatever the world may think."

"But my father—my good name?"

"What is he to your husband? And your good name—I thought you said you would die for him."

"Ah, this is worse than death, Mrs. Booth."

"Childish nonsense! And for this babyish stuff, you would make him lose his position?"

"I do not understand you."

"Who will respect him when he has for a wife the discarded and suspected daughter of a French teacher at a school in Bincester?"

"My father is a count in his own land," said Valerie, proudly.

The old woman laughed a short, sharp laugh.

"That will be a poor recommendation to my old master! He might forgive his marrying the child of an English beggar in the streets, but not the daughter of a French king."

"Ah me, what is to be done?" sighed Valerie. "But perhaps when my Reginald comes home he will let me tell papa, and then we can wait patiently. I do not value even my good name so much as Reginald's happiness."

"Pshaw! Don't you know that your father will be only too delighted to blurt out the secret. It isn't every man whose daughter can marry a Balfern."

Valerie felt that her father's pride would rebel against the concealment. The future looked very dark.

"Do you think," said the old woman after a pause, "that I was not born and educated for something better than a nurse's place? My father was a clergyman who took pupils. I was clandestinely married to one of them—the heir to a title. I knew that the discovery of our union would be his ruin, and I never claimed to be acknowledged his wife. He died five years afterwards, but I did not seek recognition by his family. Other women, you see, can do what you are called upon to do."

Now this story was partly true and partly false. It was true in the main, it was false in all the important particulars. Mrs. Booth's father was a clergyman and took pupils, and Mrs. Booth had been secretly engaged to one of them, but he was only the son of a wealthy tradesman, and had jilted her after he went to college. Her father had become a bankrupt, had his gown taken from him for some questionable practices, and died in the debtors' jail. This was why Mrs. Booth had been obliged to go into service as a nurse.

But her story and her conversation were enough to make poor Valerie miserable. Still, however, the young wife hoped for the best, and looked for Reginald's coming as the cure for all her doubts and difficulties.

In due time Valerie's child was born—a little girl. Ah, what comfort there was in that child! The mother seemed to gather fresh strength and hope from looking into her baby's eyes. It delighted Mrs. Booth to see how wrapt up Valerie was in it, for she thought that it would usurp its father's place in her heart, and make the resignation of him easier; but she somewhat miscalculated in this, as she discovered one day when she overheard Valerie talking to the little thing.

"Would they have me give you no father, darling? Oh, no, no! I would sacrifice myself, but not you, you poor little helpless angel. Heaven give me strength and life to watch over you."

Then Mrs. Booth saw that she must change her

12

tactics. She resolved to adopt a new plan; she must work on the mother through her child. And a very cruel plan it was that she devised.

When Valerie was growing stronger, she came one day, and sat down beside her on the bed.

"My dear," she said, "now that your trouble is over, and you have a child to love, I had better tell you everything; you must be prepared for the worst."

Valerie leant forward with starting eyeballs—speechless, trembling, faint with terror.

"You have been deceived. Captain Balfern cannot recognize you as his wife."

"*Cannot* recognize me?"

"No; for you are not really his wife; the ceremony was not legally performed; I have his own authority."

"Oh, impossible, impossible!" cried poor Valerie, flinging herself down on the pillow, and bursting into tears.

"It was not an intentional deception," said Mrs. Booth, who could not, even to do him a service, make Reginald appear criminal; "but it is a barrier, an insurmountable barrier, to your ever being acknowledged; in fact, you cannot be acknowledged what you are *not*—his wife."

"But he loves me so dearly; I know he loves me; he will not desert me, for I *am* his wife; a mere oversight in the ceremony cannot be so fatal to our happiness."

"Cannot desert you! What has he done now?

Did he not leave you to the certain shame of discovery, and to the wrath of your father? Did he not bind you with a solemn vow to conceal the only thing that could save you? Does this look like love—like the affection of a fond husband?"

Valerie groaned. All this was terribly true. She had tried again and again not to think so; but the old woman's words came home irresistibly to her mind.

"My child, my poor fatherless child, what will become of you?"

"Oh, the child will be provided for, and so will you, no doubt, dear. You're not the only woman who has suffered and been deceived. I have no doubt Captain Balfern will place his child where it will be well cared for, and send it to school when it grows up."

Valerie hugged her baby to her breast.

"No, no, my treasure! my darling! I have bought you at a price, and they shall not take you from me."

"Well, if you don't want to have it taken away, you had better let no one know where you are."

And then this hard old woman, with her handsome face, as stern as if it were chiselled out of stone, left the room, and poor Valerie went through her dark hour alone.

Mrs. Booth had triumphed.

Time rolled on, and no news of Reginald came. The old woman was delighted at this at first, for it made her case stronger, and gave her poison time to work. But presently she became alarmed. She received her pension quarterly through the commander of the coast-guard station, and there was generally a short letter from the Admiral with it. He too was anxious about his son. At last he wrote that he feared he was either dead or a prisoner, for his vessel had been captured by the French.

She did not speak of this to Valerie, who had ceased now to ask about her husband. As Mrs. Booth had represented to her friends and acquaintance at Halborough that Valerie was a niece of hers, whose intellects were weak, and who had had "a misfortune," the poor girl had no opportunity of hearing any news from any one else, for she was generally avoided or taken no notice of.

Valerie's little girl grew up a delicate and strange child. She had no playfellows, and was always with her mother, until she was old enough to be allowed to go out on the beach by herself. She had the sea for a playfellow then, for she did not care to make friends with the other children she met there. They were too rough and rude in their gambols for her. She used to sit on the sand-hills, looking at the distant ships dreamily, and singing some little French air that she had learnt from her mother, with her tiny treble. The people of Halborough gave her a wide birth, for they were a superstitious people, and fancied there was something elfish about her, with her strange songs, and her beautiful golden hair, and large grey eyes.

Next to the sea, she loved the picture over the

mantelpiece of the bedroom. "That little girl was so quiet and nice that she wished she would come and play with her," she said.

As may be imagined, poor Valerie had little enough money. She and Mrs. Booth had to pinch sorely to make both ends meet, and, as a consequence, poor little Aimée had but few toys or childish treasures. It was only natural that when she saw other little folk in possession of beautiful dolls, she should sigh at times for something like them. And then her mother would tell her that she should have one "when her ship came home."

By degrees, Aimée began to look forward to that event, and to connect it with a great many things.

"Mamma, will my little girl in the picture come and play with me when the ship comes home?" she asked one day. And her mother covered her with kisses, and told her some fond foolish story about the little girl, and how she was sailing in the ship, and what a beautiful ship it was, and how full of riches, and that they were all for this pet Aimée of mamma's.

How often the child's prattle wrung the poor mother's heart! There was once a terrible anguish for poor Valerie in the little one's words. It was during the summer, when Halborough could boast its visitors and made believe it was a watering place. Valerie and the child were sitting on the sand-hills, the mother working, and Aimée at her usual occupation, watching the sails in the offing, and wondering whether any of them belonged to her vessel.

A merry group of little ones passed by, frolicking and laughing round their father. "Papa, papa," was constantly on their lips, and was carried by their cheery voices to where the two were sitting on the sand-hills. Aimée looked very thoughtful as she watched them, and then, turning to her mother, said, "Mamma, other little girls have papas, haven't I got a papa? Where is he?"

Valerie was almost choked with the effort to repress her anguish. She could not speak.

"Will he come, too, when the ship comes, mamma? Oh! how I wish I could see it sailing in, with its purple silk sails, and its gold mast, and its fluttering flags. Will papa come with the ship, mamma?"

"Yes, darling, yes—I hope. I cannot tell—I hope," and Valerie turned away, for the big tears, that would not be denied, were rolling down her cheeks.

"Think of that, dolly," said Aimée to her poor old battered wooden doll, "when the ship comes home, papa will bring us such lots of fine things. And you shall have such grand dresses, dolly, and though there will be great fine wax dolls, like the little girl's at Seaview Villa, I'll love you best still—next to mamma, dolly."

Aimée was five years old now, but there was still no news of Captain Balfern. If there had been, of course, Mrs. Booth would not have told Valerie.

But the Admiral had been dead a couple of years now, and his widow, though she still remitted the pension, as directed in his will, did not trouble herself to write to Mrs. Booth, so that the old woman was really ignorant of what had happened to Reginald.

Valerie had ceased to look for his return—perhaps to care for it. She had had years to brood over the past, and his selfishness had become revealed to her. She knew that he had deliberately sacrificed her—her honour—perhaps her life, and that of his child—in order to save himself from discomforts comparatively light, when considered beside the misery to which he was knowingly condemning her.

Her whole existence was wrapt up in her child now. She had no thought, no hope, except for her.

In the winter of the year in which Aimée's sixth birthday fell, there came a time of distress and trial for the little village of Halborough. In the spring there had been some very heavy and high tides, and the embankment of the cornlands had been broken through, and all the country was under water.

Next, the sprat fishery failed, but that was of little moment after all, for the fish were chiefly sold as manure for the now flooded fields. And then there were very few visitors, for the floods frightened them away, Halborough having been an island for two whole months at the beginning of the summer. When the winter came, came the tribulation. The inhabitants of this little place always kept up a hand-to-hand fight with starvation—they were engaged all the spring and summer in laying by store for the winter—and this year there had been nothing to lay by. The farmers round about, who were the rich people of the neighbourhood, had all been ruined by the inundation, so the little village had to stand and face the famine alone and unassisted.

With the autumn, and the dense cold fogs which it sucked up from the marshes, came sickness—as usual. But this time the people were too enfeebled by privation, by want of food, and clothing, and fuel, to withstand its ravages. The sickness was in the village all the autumn and on into the winter, and the churchyard at the back of the town at the edge of the marshes—so near the edge that some of the graves were half full of water within an hour after they were dug—was covered with fresh heaps of black mould, for the people had not the time or the heart to turf them.

One of the first victims of the sickness was old Mrs. Booth. It was not that she was suffering so severely from want as many of her neighbours, for the pension was enough to guard her against that. But she was frightened at the illness all round. She tried all sorts of preventives, never moved out of doors, and was in a constant state of terror lest she should run risk of infection. The result was that she frightened herself into an illness which soon took an alarming turn, passed rapidly into the prevalent fever, one of a typhoid character, and the old woman died before the doctor could be summoned from Bradshall. There was no resident surgeon, and Bradshall was nearly four miles off.

When Mrs. Booth felt death approaching, you may be sure that she did not look back upon her treatment of Valerie with much complacency. A deathbed is the only place in which some people can judge justly of their own actions; but it is, alas! too late to repair the wrongs then. Sorely, sorely did the old woman suffer remorse for her conduct; and with it there mingled a terrible doubt that after all Reginald might have loved Valerie very truly. He might, even now, be longing to find her, wondering where she was, and broken-hearted at her loss. But it was too late. She had not even the strength to tell Valerie of the deception she had practised on her. All that she could do, just as the world was closing to her, and her soul was on the point of taking its flight, was to clasp Valerie's hand, and whisper, "I did all for the best—I did all for the best."

The old woman was buried, and the fact of her death reported by the commander of the coastguard to Lady Balfern. He also mentioned that Mrs. Booth had left her niece and child, as he supposed, unprovided for. Lady Balfern, however, was not the sort of woman to trouble herself about that. "We have had to keep the old hag long enough, we can't be expected to provide for all her relations," she said, as she tossed the note into the fire. Mrs. Booth had left Balfern House long before her ladyship married Sir Matthew.

Then came hard times for poor Valerie. The shop, as has been already mentioned, drove but a very small trade, and her stock of money was slender. After a hard struggle, she had long ago sold some of the contents of the jewel-casket, and now one by one the more precious relics which she had laid aside had to be parted with.

She and Aimée had to live on very poor fare. The winter was but just begun, and the jewels, which she got miserable prices for, would hardly carry them through the trying time. Aimée was always a delicate and sickly child. Visitors to Halborough as they passed her with their groups of healthy, rosy children, looked at her pityingly and exchanged glances full of meaning. Sometimes an unguarded whisper would reach Valerie's ear— "Poor little thing, there's death in that face!" Then she would snatch her child to her heart, gaze into her dear face, and try to read the doom which others saw there. But it was kindly veiled from her. She kissed the little white brow, and did not see the seal set there. She looked into the eyes, but did not perceive the strange fatal light in them. She smoothed the pale cheek, and did not feel the deadly damp; she toyed with the golden curls, and never saw that their brightness was borrowed from the light of another world.

When the winter set in, Aimée could no longer take her walk to the beach, or sit on her favourite sand-hills to look for the promised sail. But she used to sit at the window of the bed-room from which she could catch a glimpse of the sea. There she would stay for hours, and her mother, who now occupied the little room behind the shop, used to hear her incessantly talking to "her little girl in the picture."

By and by poor Aimée was too tired to sit at the window. She used to lie on her bed, with her eyes fixed on the portrait over the mantelpiece; sometimes talking to it, and sometimes singing snatches of song in her low voice. "I am so tired, mamma," was her constant complaint.

She was sickening. Her mother saw it, with what alarm can be readily imagined. She sent for the doctor, but he only shook his head, and ordered a nourishing diet and wine. Then the jewel-casket was once more in requisition, and what she had hoped to make last for the winter was sold at once. The jeweller at Bradshall to whom she sent them, was astonished at the beauty of a large topaz which was among them, but he paid her none the more handsomely for his astonishment.

Poor Valerie, friendless, helpless, and hopeless, it was no wonder that she turned to her father now. She wrote him a long, sorrowful letter, and implored his aid, not for herself but her child. She received no answer!

Aimée did not improve at all. She shrank almost to a skeleton, although Valerie procured the most nourishing food she could for her, while she herself, poor mother, lived upon dry bread. She determined to husband every shilling in order to purchase what was necessary for her child, and to pay for medical attendance.

Dr. Stanforth, her physician, was a poor man with a large family, and could not afford to attend patients for nothing. Besides, he never saw, although her house was a humble one, any signs of poverty about, and she seemed of so superior a rank in life that he never suspected her of being in want. So he took his guinea a visit, never dreaming how ill she could spare it,—though she never begrudged it, for was it not for her darling's safety?

And now all the jewels were sold, and the money was going so fast, she determined to search and see what there might be belonging to Mrs. Booth that she could convert into money. Almost the first thing she came upon was a box containing letters; one of them, written in Reginald's hand, caught her eye. She opened and read it. It was the one in which he had told Mrs. Booth to prepare for his wife's arrival. It was evident from this letter that Mrs. Booth had deceived her. She was, indeed, Reginald's wife, and he intended to acknowledge her on his father's death. But the discovery came too late to revive Valerie's love for him. She only saw in his solicitude for her comfort here, a selfish solicitude; she could detect selfishness now even in the very expression of his love for her.

In another letter she read of the Admiral's anxiety about the prolonged absence of his son, and his fear that he was either dead or a prisoner. When she had finished, she looked toward the bed where Aimée was lying asleep.

"For her sake—for our child's sake—Reginald, dead or alive, you will absolve me from a portion of my vow."

And she sat down and wrote once again to her father. For the first time she told him of her being really married; but she did not reveal her husband's name; she said she could not do so yet; but she entreated him to have pity—to come to her—to save a far dearer life than hers. Then, having dispatched her letter, she knelt by her child's bed and prayed to be supported and granted patience and strength until she received a reply.

That night Aimée was worse; she tossed in feverish restlessness, and next morning seemed worn out. All through her delirium Valerie had heard her calling to the little girl in the picture, and asking her to come and put her cool hand on her hot forehead.

When Doctor Stanforth came she told him of this. He looked at the picture and said, "There's something odd about the expression of it; it's an old painting—a family portrait, I suppose. Perhaps it would be as well to turn its face to the wall till my little patient is better. In fever, even a staring pattern in a paper is injurious."

So the picture was turned to the wall. That night Aimée still continued delirious; but poor Valerie was so wearied with continuous watching that she could keep awake no longer. She dozed fitfully in her chair, too worn out to move or to do more than look to see that her child was safe in the bed. She never knew whether she was really awake or asleep, but about the middle of the night it appeared to her that she was roused by the child's talking and laughing. Aimée was speaking to the little girl in the picture, and Valerie's impression was that, looking towards the mantelpiece, she saw the picture, in the bright moonlight, turned round again with its back to the wall. Next morning, however, she found it as she had left it the night before; but Aimée was still weaker and fainter. For two days the child kept fading and fading; and yet no news from her father.

At last the money failed. On the third day, when Dr. Stanforth visited her, she had only a guinea in this world, and that was his fee!

He was struck with the change in the child.

"Good Heavens! this cannot last long, I fear. She is sinking from sheer weakness."—Poor child, the food had run short now.—"You must try and make her take some strong beef-tea. I will ride home as quickly as I can, and send you some restoratives and tonics. This is a terrible change!"

He took his guinea, never noticing how poor Valerie had to struggle with an inclination to ask him to let her keep it, and wait a little for his fee. He mounted his horse, flinging a penny to the boy who had held it, and clattered away down the street.

With hungry eyes poor Valerie watched the urchin as he turned over the penny meditatively. She called to him—

"You are a good boy for watching the doctor's horse; see here, I'll give you all these for your penny, because you are a good boy."

She emptied a bottle of sweets into a paper, and held them out to him. They were old ones; he had known them as long as he could remember in Mrs. Booth's window, but he was to get them all for a penny, so it did not matter. He took his prize, and Valerie clutched the money and hurried out.

How carefully she carried that greasy coin. It was her last penny in the world, and she had to save her child's life. She went to the butcher's shop in the higher part of the town. Business was very slack even with him now. A poor neck of mutton and a spare leg of beef was all that he had to display. Valerie walked by the shop twice before she could summon the courage to enter; but the recollection of the poor pale little face on the pillow at home nerved her, and she went in. The butcher was seated on the chopping-block, whistling gloomily, and cutting up a skewer for want of employment.

"Will you sell me—a pennyworth of meat, please? It's for my bird,—and it likes beef best."

The butcher stared at her—chopped a ragged end off the beef and flung it towards her. She caught it up, laid down the penny, and hurried from the shop.

"That crazy niece of old Mrs. Booth's, eh! I wonder how she gets on now her aunt's dead." said the butcher, resuming his seat and his occupation.

Valerie hastened home, and taking a peep at her child, went down to prepare the beef-tea with the poor scrap of meat she had purchased. How tedious the process seemed. The tiny teacupful of water stood simmering slowly, it seemed an hour. She kept running up and down between the bedroom and the kitchen, trembling with anxiety and terror. For she could not but see that poor Aimée was sinking faster and still faster.

Don't smile for Heaven's sake, dear reader, but it was positively a race between the child's life and that necessarily slow process of cooking!

At last, however, the beef-tea was ready, and Valerie poured it into a cup, which she stood in a bowl of cold water to cool it. And then she hurried up with it to the child's room.

As she opened the door she saw Aimée sitting up in the bed. "Mamma, mamma! my little girl is here to play with me, so the ship has come home, mamma,—the ship has come home at last."

And then the weary head fell back on the pillow, with its golden profusion of curls. One soft sigh, a smile, as the darkening eyes turned towards Valerie—and the little spirit was free, and fluttered up from that dark, desolate chamber into God's presence, and all the brightness of Heaven.

"Oh, my darling, my treasure!" and Valerie

was kneeling by the bedside clasping the poor little corpse to her heart as if she could cling to the life that was gone, and retain it. But it was only the empty casket of her jewel that she held, and even the fire that was consuming her heart could not warm it into existence.

She was obliged to yield to the bitter knowledge at last, and then stunned and numb with the mental agony she rose from her knees, and sat on the edge of the bed, clasping the tiny dead hand, lost to everything, save the recollection of her child, and insensible to all outward sights and sounds.

*　　*　　*　　*　　*

Valerie's father after she left him became even more reserved and self-contained than before. He saw no one, spoke to no one, save his pupils and those who employed him.

He was a broken-spirited, miserable old man, and only kept alive by the old fire of his pride. But for that he must have succumbed. He was determined that no one should suspect him of grieving for one who had dishonoured him.

When Valerie's first letter reached him, he burst into a fit of ungovernable rage. "Was it not bad enough that she reminded him of her dishonoured existence, but that she must tell him that she had sold the de Lavalle jewels to support the child of her shame!" and the old man cursed his daughter again.

The second letter was as ineffectual as the first. He would not believe that she was married. "A liar! The first de Lavalle that was a liar; she only employed the talents of her race to make her falsehood seem like truth!" And he cursed her yet again.

The day after this last letter reached him, a stranger came to Mrs. Martin's, inquired for Valerie, and insisted on seeing Monsieur Delaval. He was a wild odd-looking man, clothed in rags, and with a beard as unkempt as a lion's mane. He would take no refusal, but forced himself into the old man's presence.

"Your daughter, Monsieur Delaval, where is your daughter?"

It was enough! The old man instinctively guessed who was his questioner. He sprang to the mantel-shelf, snatched down the broken blade of his sword, and flung himself madly on the stranger.

"Wretch, betrayer, dishonourer of the race of de Lavalle, die!" he shrieked, as he lunged fiercely at his throat.

But the aged arm was nerveless. The stranger —he was Reginald Balfern—put it aside with ease, caught the broken weapon, and flung it behind him.

"Fool—weak old fool! Where is your daughter —where is my wife?"

At that Monsieur Delaval hesitated.

"Your wife?"

"Yes, my wife; mine, Reginald Balfern—Sir Reginald, if you like—curse all titles, and all money, and all rank—my wife, if you and I haven't murdered her between us. Where is she?"

But the father had fallen in a heap on the floor, with his head against the wall.

"*Mon Dieu! Mon Dieu!* and she was innocent!"

But Reginald Balfern was too fiercely moved to suffer him to lie there. He dragged him up, held him against the wall, and once again hissed his question into his face from between his clenched teeth.

"Where is she?"

And then the old man, as best he could gather his scattered senses, related hurriedly all that had happened. When he spoke of the two appealing letters, a fierce fire glittered in Reginald's eye, and he cried—

"Great God, you have murdered my child."

"And what have you done to mine?" asked the old man.

Reginald groaned.

"Let us in Heaven's name do all we can to repair the wrong. How far—how far? Order a chaise and pair at once." He rushed to the bell, and rang it until Mrs. Martin appeared. "Order a chaise and pair, the fastest pair in the stables at once."

Mrs. Martin hesitated.

"I order it—Sir Reginald Balfern, of Balfern Hall,—will that satisfy you? Curse the woman she'd stand there staring while my wife and child are dying!"

Through all the strangeness of his appearance there was something of the old Reginald visible, and Mrs. Martin recognized it, and obeyed his orders.

Before long, Monsieur Delaval and Reginald were tearing along the road to Halborough as fast as two horses could gallop.

Reginald Balfern had been nearly seven years a captive in a French prison. In the solitude of that long confinement he had had time to reflect on his past, and his character became softened by adversity. A real and deep love for his wife took the place of his old half-selfish admiration of and pride in her. And he bitterly repented the misery he had, as he knew only too well, entailed upon her.

When at length he obtained his freedom, he flew without a moment's delay to find her. He had been put ashore on the point of the Essex bank of the Thames nearest to Bincester, and had hurried at once across country to find her or her father.

And now at length he was on the road to clasp her once more to his heart and ask her pardon!

*   *   *   *   *

Valerie, sitting by the deathbed of Aimée, did not take note of hasty footsteps on the stairs,—was only roused from her unconsciousness by the sight of her father and her husband — she recognized him at a glance—as they rushed into the room.

But she never moved, or changed colour. She was ashy pale—she was stone-cold—she seemed as dead as the child beside her.

They were terrified at her immobility, and paused on the threshold.

Her father rushed forward, and falling at her feet cried out in broken accents—"My child, my child!"

She did not turn her head, but the white lips moved mechanically, and she answered, "*My child, my* child!"

Her husband knelt beside her, and seizing her listless right hand, covered it with warm kisses and warm tears. But in her left lay the tiny hand of her dead child. And the chill from it smote her heart, and she remained stern, implacable, passionless as a statue.

Then the two men shrank from her in fear and anguish, and, leaning on each other's shoulders, wept like children.

*   *   *   *   *

Lady Balfern is a fine handsome woman. But hers are eyes that have looked into the eyes of Sorrow.

The sea closes above a sunken vessel, and its surface bears no recording ripple. The billowy green turf of the churchyard swallows up the dead and shows no sign. But a happiness gone down at sea, a buried grief, leaves an indelible epitaph graven on the human brow, leaves an undying memorial lamp that burns in the eyes of those who have suffered and survived.

And if the features are thus marked, how is the poor heart scarred—wounds of warfare deeply seamed and only to be effaced when death's hand crumbles the earthen casket whereon they are written!

Lady Balfern is beloved for her acts of charity, but she is reserved and silent, and even those who bless her have seldom seen her.

It is supposed that she and her husband, Sir Reginald, live no less happily together than other married people.

She has several children.

She is an exemplary wife—an exemplary mother.

But at night, when the little ones are gone to bed and the nursery is deserted, Valerie, Lady Balfern, takes a key from a jewel-casket, which contains nothing beside, and going to the nursery, unlocks a cupboard there.

In that cupboard there lie a child's clothes, of very coarse material, carefully folded, with a pair of little shoes on the top of them. Beside them you will see a mere log of a wooden doll, legless and armless, dressed in a common duster, tied round it with an old shoe-string; a headless horse, with red spots; and a little wooden spade, worn-out with much digging.

This is what the Key of the Nursery Cupboard has to reveal.

THE KEY OF THE STUDY.

THE KEY OF THE STUDY.

There is still, upon the table of the study, a plain old writing-case, with here and there some dark stains upon it that have been there for years, which no one has effaced or will seek to efface. As the dull night closes in, and the thickening gloom of the shadows fills the room, a big man, bearded and brown, sits wearily by the hearth, smoking, and gazing intently at the fire. Pictures enough he sees there, but in not one of them any hope for the future—in not one of them any consolation; for the pictures are all pictures of a past whose soul and life have gone out of him, leaving him in middle age thus lonely and thus miserable. And yet, as he looks, he seems to see, wistfully regarding him from the very heart of the fire, a face, no longer indeed bright and cheerful, but sombre in its melancholy beauty, which might make him very happy even now but for stern restrictions and restraints. Soon the image fades away, and in its place comes that of an old man, grey-haired, and with an awful look of pain in the dark eyes; and he turns with a dull sob from the fire to the table with the writing-case. No need to tell *him* what the stains mean, for there again passes through his soul the misery, acute and sudden, of a night long ago. Outside the old house the wind is rising.

We change the scene.

The theatre is full, and there is a burst of plaudits as the great actress sweeps upon the stage, with her long black tresses floating negligently behind, with her dark eyes fixed and solemn; and again there is a burst of plaudits when the wonderful voice, the voice that seems almost breaking with its heavy burden of passion long suppressed, fills the great house with the glory of its sound. She can play upon a thousand hearts as the artist on his violin can touch what string he likes, and make it vibrate tremulously at his will. But as for her *own* heart, can she rule *that?* When the play is over, when she has reached *her* home, see how wearily she too sinks into her chair by the fireside. Once only she rouses herself from her dull lethargy; it is when her husband enters the room: and then, petulantly, not with the strong sweet accents that have so sovereignly swayed the crowd, but with almost the peevishness of a sick girl, she tells him she is weary, and implores him to be gone. For her, too, there are pictures in the fire.

From whence had they started, this broken man, this broken woman? The story is a long one; it takes us back twenty years. Of the three persons named, only two then knew each other; the third, you perceive, the husband, intrudes. Let us get away from that lonely study, in which the soldier still broods over his grief; let us get away from the actress's home, where she mourns over the past; let us get out into the open air, and take the story up where it began, just twenty years ago.

Captain Grant, who had served with much honour in India and elsewhere, was then a widower, forty-five years of age, and with one son, Donald, a lad of eighteen. He lived in an old house, that had been inhabited by his family for many generations, in Argyleshire, not far from the shores of Loch Awe, and his life was happy enough, for, after much hard fighting and many wounds, he was yet alert and hale, and saw his son growing up from a glorious boy into a glorious man. The youngster had never left that lonely but beautiful region, nor had he yet felt any desire for a different life. There was no keener angler, no surer shot, in the whole county. The mere physical enjoyment of existence was vouchsafed him in full measure, and it was spiritualized, too, by an intense love for natural beauty. The mystery of the lonely tarn, the wierd wonder of the mountain mist, the glory of a Highland cataract roaring in flood, and the luxury of the purple heather—all these thrilled him with a vague delight, which was the more powerful because he had as yet no morbid anxiety to know its source. Very noble was the love between father and son; both were so proud of each other, both could trust each other so thoroughly. As they strode along over the moors, gun in hand, you could hardly see two finer types of manhood. The father knew no reason why his happiness should be disturbed, for it was *then* purest when his son shared it with him. Captain Grant had lived hard in his time; his youth had been stormy and passionate; but at length he was won over to a better life by the lady whom he married, and there had since been only one heavy cloud upon him; it was that which darkened his home when she died. But now this also had passed away into a tender and gentle memory, which lent an inexpressible charm to his affection for his son. To keep this son out of temptations under which he himself had often fallen—to rear him into a gallant gentleman, pure, and truthful, and brave—these were the Captain's aims, and for eighteen years he had no fear of their realization.

Of late, however, there was something in the lad's manner which, to eyes that saw keenly because love lent them force, denoted a critical change; and the Captain beheld it with a certain glee, if also with a certain fear. He knew its meaning, did this good gentleman; he knew that his son must have discovered the existence in our charming world of a beauty which beats that of tarn, moorland, and stream.

Now the Captain, having had his own experiences in these matters, was not surprised to find that the boy was often melancholy without seeming cause; that he grew, in fact, a little less earnest about salmon and grouse, and a little fonder of long walks without either rod or gun. Noticing the change, the worthy old warrior did not ask himself the question,

"What *is* it?"

The worthy old warrior only asked himself the question,

"Who is *she*?"

Whereupon, taking counsel with himself alone, as became a good gentleman who had seen much of the world and its ways, he revolved within his brain the names of all the "eligible young ladies" in the district whom his son had seen. He knew enough to believe that an early marriage to a true helpmeet is the grandest happiness that a young man can have, and is also his stoutest shield against evil and sorrow. If Donald were in love with Lucy Stewart, or Flora Lennox, or any other Scotch maiden whose father's lands lay near his own, and whose blood was as pure as that of the Grants themselves, why there could be no earthly cause to prevent Donald, after a few years, from marrying her. He could have wished that the lad would tell him at once; but he knew that young love is seldom confidential at its commencement—that it broods upon itself, and finds something very sacred in its secrecy. So, without any serious misgivings, the father waited until his son, who hitherto had kept nothing hidden from him, should ask his aid in this matter also.

In which position of affairs there existed the elements of great happiness for both of them, *if* Donald had selected an "eligible young lady."

If, on the contrary, Donald had *not*, well, there was the chance of an awkward explosion; for the Captain, with all his affection, had in him great faculties of anger, and the fierce family pride of a Highland squire. But as yet he had no reason to believe that Donald had made any unworthy choice. The lad had been kept free from the dangers of a city; and the Captain knew, from the clear bright eyes which met him so frankly and so lovingly every day—he knew, from his son's ruddy cheeks, from the eager exuberant health that seemed to breathe in his every movement, that Donald was as pure as a girl in her nursery, whilst he was as strong and as brave as became the son of a soldier. Without laying traps, then, for the lad's secret, he watched that magnificent young animal's movements with a curiosity which was not absolutely free from a certain sense of amusement.

Donald Grant went up Glenorchy early one September morning. The glen is one of the loveliest in Scotland. There is nothing grand about it; none of the savage sublimity of Glencoe, for instance; it grows very fine, it is true, as it widens out towards Loch Awe, with the rugged outline of Ben Lhui on the one side, and the massive bulk of Cruachan on the other; but to any one who comes upon it after traversing the loneliness of the Black Mount or the wide waste moorland that stretches away from Glen Etive up to Loch Rannoch, it is apt to seem tame. Wander down the glen quietly, however, following the course of the stream, and you soon begin to recognize a peculiar and delicate charm about the valley. You have had your fill of ruggedness and desolation, and there is a wonderful sense of rest and peace in the rich woodlands that border the stream. Not that the Orchy is a tame and sluggish river, winding on past melancholy willows so slowly that you can scarcely tell which way it is going, if, indeed, it is going at all; no, it is always brisk and rapid, and when a night's rain has helped it, it rushes down to Loch Awe with all the speed and glory that beseem a Highland river. Thus coursed it when Donald went up along its banks. The morning was exquisitely bright. The mists that had been thronging round Cruachan for days had passed away in fantastic wreaths and curls, and in the clear air every crag of the grand old mountain seemed distinct and close. Striding along, the lad was soon some miles up the Glen, and close to the Falls. The sunshine played marvellous tricks amongst the pine trunks, and seemed absolutely to glow and burn where it struck upon the red berries of the mountain ash; musically murmured the Orchy, swelling into a more solemn song as the lad drew near the great boulders over which the river rushes to the deep pools beneath; and the sky was flooded with light, and the air was flooded with music, and the heart of the lad was flooded with love. As he paused near the cascade and looked around him, he seemed a natural part of the glorious scene. The place would have been lonely, perchance; something of its charm would have gone out of it had it lacked that tall young fellow with the keen bright eyes that glanced about so eagerly—with the long golden hair that danced so merrily, with the manly form, the broad shoulders, the long arms; with the bonnet on his brow, gay with sprigs of heather, on which the dew was still wet; with the long folds of the kilt falling into new shapes at every movement of the supple limbs. Health, and strength, and Highland air, and eighteen—if anybody could not be content with these, he would be hard to satisfy!

Yes; but there is something wanting still. Such a glorious young lover needs a mate.

It all depends upon circumstances whether the reader will believe that at the distant glimpse of A Gown, the sunshine became at least twenty times more bright and beautiful; that the mavis, and merle, and throstle, and a host of other choristers, all began to sing away as if for dear life, almost choking their delicate little throats in their wild and ecstatic hurry to pour out the largest possible number of notes in the smallest possible number of minutes; that the waterfall suddenly glowed with a kaleidoscopic iridescence of exuberant colour compared to which a hundred double rainbows would have seemed like a dull cloak of hodden grey— that there went rushing through the boy's veins a torrent of passion to which Niagara is Dutch, and that then his soul reached a serene elevation to which the top of Chimborazo is the bottom of a coal-pit.

Yes; if the reader *has* been ever deliciously mad, he (for we must not talk of *she*) will understand all this. Yes, he knows that it is impossible to grow extravagant or hyperbolical about That Young Lady!

Poor Donald Grant!

Mary Horton was *not* a young lady.

No; but she was very beautiful, and looked all the more so perchance because her beauty was so different from his own. The subtlest harmonies, whether of sight or sound, are those that spring from contrast. The lad was handsome, with the ruddy colour of the North; his long hair was golden, but with a glow in it warmer than that of gold; the girl, again, had the dark tresses, the deep eyes, eloquent, fiery, intense, of the South. His was the grace, the beauty of aggression; hers, though as passionate as his, seemed pleading and submissive! As he stooped down, so that they looked each other fairly in the face, he seemed like some Norse rover who had travelled, let us say, in Spain, and did not intend to return to Norway alone! Their eyes met; they told each other so much more than the few stammering words of greeting, that the girl turned her head aside, trembling a little at the eager glance which seemed to devour her secret with an almost cruel triumph.

She was not a lady, as we have said; she was the orphan daughter of very poor people; she was—the melancholy fact must be admitted—only a lady's-maid. A clever girl was Mary Horton; too romantic, no doubt; had chiefly nourished her brain upon novels; and saw in Donald as fine a young hero as any Reginald De Courcy, or Alured de Bohun who had ever, for love's sake, married " a damsel of low degree." Poor, little girl! With such splendid possibilities in her, with such eyes, such a voice, she was not over-safe in a world where men are selfish often in the very degree of their passion. She knew this, too, in a dim way; and her dreams were often sorely troubled when the ladies whom she served had dismissed her for the night. Were these novels *true*, that she had read so eagerly? She hoped they might be; but—but —but she could hardly hope that the gentleman would be true to her. Besides, was she fit for him, fit to be his wife? There again, poor little Mary, knowing her own deficiences, felt herself very helpless and forlorn. It is lucky for girls that they can cry!

And yet she was safe enough with Donald Grant. Had that young gentleman been able to do so, which he was *not*, he would then and there have married her off-hand.

Would the union have been a happy one, after all? Well, there would probably have been troubles, and difficulties, and sorrows, which their young heads had never thought of. Meanwhile, it was very sweet to be thus alone together.

* * * * *

Two hours after this, an observant and intelligent Scottish man of the menial persuasion, received from Captain Grant two things: number one, a guinea for valuable information; number two, a kick for having played the spy. He accepted both with serene imperturbability.

No one in the Captain's house had a pleasant time of it that day; and at dinner, Donald could see that something had crossed his father, whilst the father could see that his son was ill at ease.

The Captain suffered least; for his morality, after all, was little more than the conventional code of honour prevalent amongst men of the world; whereas the poor lad was horribly in earnest. Nay, if we were to anatomize the old campaigner's feelings very deeply, we might discover that the *amourette*—for he could not believe that it was anything more serious—really vexed him very little. Boys would be boys; this girl, who was said to be so pretty, must be easily got out of the way, and so on, and so on; wronging all the while two people, one of whom was inexpressibly dear to him, and both of whom were pure. Perhaps, thought he, it was not worth while to open the campaign in force; he would get Donald out of this dangerous neighbourhood, of course; "calf-love" was not at all unnatural, and did not usually last very long.

Thus mused the old campaigner, and on the whole resolved not to commence the attack just yet, but to remain within his trenches.

Imagine the veteran's dismay when, of a sudden, the enemy dashed into his lines!

"I—I want to speak to you, sir, very seriously!"

quoth the audacious Donald. The shock was over; the surprise was over; it had been a severe one, and the Captain was annoyed to find that in the confusion of the attack, he had absolutely spilled a glass of claret; but now he was on his guard, and a great deal cooler than the assailant.

The rebel force was evidently embarrassed; there was plenty of pluck about it, but very little discipline. In fact, it at once endeavoured to deprive the inevitable conflict of its most sanguinary features.

"You have always been a very good father to me, sir," cries Rebel, not at all in a determined manner.

"Well, my dear boy, I hope so," answers British Veteran, seeing his advantage, and quietly massing his forces against the weakest point of the enemy's line. "I hope so, Donald. Surely *that's* not the very serious business?"

"No, sir; but—but, you know, sir, I'm past eighteen."

"Delightful age!" replies the Captain, "and really, paternal vanity apart, Donald, I never met with a finer young gentleman at that period of life. Come, my boy, out with it. It can hardly be *very* serious after all, I fancy — not likely to prevent you from trying the Deep Pool with me to-morrow morning, eh?"

By this admirable strategic manœuvre, the great tactician indicated, without ostentatiously announcing, his knowledge of the enemy's movements.

"Indeed, sir, it *is* very serious."

Now, Donald had carefully rehearsed a clever speech; and had Donald's father committed the enormous mistake of being angry, that speech would doubtless have been delivered; but as matters befell, Donald, not without an unpleasant suspicion that he was rather mismanaging a case which had seemed delightfully clear early in the day, could only stammer forth—

"The fact is, sir, I'm in love!"

And, to his utter discomfiture, replied the Captain—

"My dear, dear boy, do you think I didn't know that already?"

There was nothing for it now but a plain confession, and a plain confession it was, which the father heard with a growing pain as the son went on with a growing earnestness. But then the captain changed his tactics, and fought sternly; the danger was more serious than he had thought, and, as his last word, he uttered an absolute and peremptory "No!"

"God help me, then," cried the lad. "I must do my duty. Indeed, sir, if you could only see her—if you could only know how good she is?"

"Be good enough, Donald, to remember that you are talking to a gentleman, and that I can't go to look for my son's wife in a servants' hall. I deal with you plainly; I will *not* have the thing spoken of again, Donald. It must cease, sir, now and for ever."

And here the battle ended; for, with a stormy sob, the boy rose from his seat and left the room.

He was miserable enough, but he was not half so miserable as his father, who still sat at the table, with strange pangs torturing him, and a dreary fear of the future at his heart. This boy whom he so loved—of whom he was so passionately proud—this boy to fling away the prospects of a life for a pair of black eyes! He would not have it; and yet how nervously he shrank from another unkind word!

Then when it grew late, he went sorrowfully to his son's room.

The boy was asleep, but sleeping uneasily, and at times indistinctly muttering words whose meaning the Captain fancied he could guess. Then the Captain's heart yearned again towards his son; and as, after he had silently and solemnly blessed him, he prepared to go, a gentle smile passed over the boy's face. He woke, and saw his father beside him; then first, ere he was quite conscious, he lovingly held out his hand for the familiar farewell clasp, and then remembering, turned away his head, crying bitterly.

But not so bitterly as his father, who, cut to the very heart by the sight of this sorrow, bent over the boy's bed and kissed him, so that their tears mingled, and their souls too, and besought him, in the broken tones which are so terrible to hear when a grown man utters them, to be wiser.

And what he could not have done by mere persuasion, nor by mere exercise of will, he did by this great grief of his! And though the lad groaned as he gave his promise, he promised that he would in all things obey his father as before.

*	*	*	*	*

Then there was peace between father and son; but after a civil war you don't find people settling down quietly to their old avocations. The old order can't be restored by a proclamation; the struggle has left wounds that throb and rankle—heart-burnings which cannot be stilled. When the two next met there was a difference in their bearing. The old entire and utter confidence and love were gone; in its stead there were other feelings, stronger and more intense, but less pure, less spontaneous. Each knew that this change had come over their relationship; each was angry with himself, grieved at the other; each was determined not to show this embarrassment; and hence both, much against their will and wish, were really awkward—talkative at the wrong season, silent at inconvenient moments.

Donald had given his promise, and never dreamt of breaking it; but there was a wild tempest of passion raging within him, and storming against his resolution. You can hardly expect Eighteen to sacrifice its first dream without something in the nature of an explosion. Now, young love is generally selfish; but let us do the boy the justice to own, that so far as *he* knew, he was angry and wild simply because he had promised to abandon *her*. What seemed his grievance was the thought of the sorrow *she* would have to go through.

She went through it very well. Women fret themselves abundantly over imaginary sorrows; give them a real grief, inflict upon them an actual pain, and they bear it much better than the lord of the creation, who is rather given to cry out in a lordly way when his pangs become acute. There was one more meeting between the lovers, whereof the Captain had full cognizance; for the son was morally a prisoner on parole, and he was a gentleman. And at this meeting, with many tears, many sobs—with wild, fiery glances of passion and unutterable murmurs of regret, the two gave up their dream. It was in the evening that they met, and at the old trysting-place; but the brightness of Glenorchy was gone. Sorrowfully they parted: and as each went homeward, the solemn mists of the night rose in the valley, and hung heavily about the mountain range. Slowly they walked away, nor for some time could either bear to look round; but at length Donald, turning, saw the girl dimly and obscurely fading into the mist, and wandering alone up the gloomy valley into the great darkness that lay beyond; and a chill touched his blood, and a dreary vision of long separation, of tender yearnings for reunion never to be fulfilled—a vision of a life barren and purposeless henceforth, passed before him. Querulously seemed the river to mourn as he walked along, and still the mists thickened.

He reached home. His father waited for him with a stern anxiety, in the fear that his last interview might have led the boy into forgetfulness of his promise. But in the forced gaiety of the son, in the strange light which gleamed from his large eyes—ay, and worse than this, in a tone of polite submission which he had never heard before from Donald's lips—the Captain knew that it was all over, that for good or evil the trial had been undergone, and that the youngster had passed sentence upon his folly. For good or for evil? Could there be any doubt of it? Of course, it was for good: and now Donald must leave the place, must see something more of the world, must have something to keep his mind from brooding over his grief. They would go to London; they would see the great city together. His own knowledge and experience would keep Donald free from many dangers. The boy acquiesced with a gallant air of cheerfulness, which did not deceive his father; and then filling a huge glass, drank as a toast, laughingly, "Goodbye to Glenorchy!"

Yes; good-bye to Glenorchy, and to all the old happy life; to the morning plunge in the burn, to the mid-day rest on the moorland; good-bye to the old peacefulness, the old perfect trust. Father and son had been one, and were two. That was all.

Except indeed that poor little Mary Horton's heart seemed breaking when this cruel, cruel end came to her poor romance.

*   *   *   *

London had upon Donald Grant the effect which London frequently has upon young gentlemen who have warm blood in their veins, and a touch of fire in their nature. London first repelled him, then attracted him, then satiated him, then wearied him, and as he went through these various phases and conditions in the order named, he naturally got a good deal altered from the lad who was ready to sacrifice all for love, except his duty to his father. He had often seen the sun rise in the Highlands; he got to be familiar with the rising of that luminary in London; the difference being merely this—that he himself in the Highlands used also to rise, and that in London he had not been to bed. Babylon has many cunning lures and artfully meshed nets; she catches young folks in her toils very easily.

But it is not *only* young folks that she catches! Captain Grant was to have guided his son; but who was to guide Captain Grant? We shall see, by and by, how it went with him. Meanwhile, this at least was certain, that his boy was no longer a boy—that he had grown into a man—and a man who was not happy. No! when the London fever began to run into its later stages, Donald had a profound contempt for his own weakness; he had wasted much and learned little; his heart was growing weary; he had tried to fill it with poor semblances of love, to no purpose; although the affection for his father had not become weaker, it had undergone a change. It was a sad time for Donald when he began to see that his father, after all, had faults and errors, which were not all of them of the generous kind so readily pardoned in youth, and so seldom repeated in age. The town life palled upon our young

Scot, who tired of wasting his years in a dull round. Society bored him; and when he went into the wilderness to kick up his heels, he found that Bohemia was quite as tiresome as society. What to do? At any rate to get away—to travel, to work, to fight, to live a life with some real excitement about it.

Captain Grant, on his part, could not but feel that it was *he* who had changed the boy, and he could not cheat himself into the belief that the change was really for the better. After all had he blundered? He could not believe *that*. He had kept Donald from "disgracing" himself by a marriage with one so far below him socially as Mary Horton; but he was fain to remember that there were other bonds of "disgrace," and that if his son was now more worldly-wise he had purchased a knowledge which did not seem to make him any happier at the expense of much nobler qualities. Somewhat tarnished was this bright boy of his; some of the London atmosphere had got into his lungs, let us say, and he did not breathe so freely.

Their house grew to be a rather sad one: and at length both felt that they would be better apart. Never an angry word passed, or could pass, between them; but there were now reserves and suppressions which were perhaps worse than positive quarrels. The Captain was almost relieved, after all, when he knew that his son was willing to go to India; the son was glad when he got a commission.

And Mary Horton? She too was in London, but she had been obliged to leave her employment, for the Captain who could pity his son had no pity for her; there were young men in the family that she served who might, said the Captain to her mistress, be deluded as Donald had been. Then when they had removed to London, they dismissed her, not unkindly, but plainly stating why. They offered her a sum of money beyond her wages; and the poor girl had to take it, though her spirit rose against the offer. She must maintain herself; she could not leave her employer's home penniless; so with a heart that was on fire with anger, she thanked them. What harm had she done? She thought. Was it her fault if Donald had loved her, and then, at a word from his father, forsaken her in her need? It was cruel, it was base, it was a shame; and then the current of her thought would change, and she would cry to herself that Donald was right. She was not fit for him; he would have had to blush for her among his friends, and she could not bear to think that Donald, so proud as he was too, should have to blush. No, it was all for the best, and as for her, she must provide for herself elsewhere.

She lost the greater part of her money very soon. Employment offices and dishonest advertisers were as plentiful then as now; and this poor girl was easily swindled. And as she drew to the end of her resources she fell ill, and first her pride would not allow her to send for help to her former mistress, who would have aided her; and then the fever and excitement of her brain told upon her, and she grew much worse.

When the poor are kind to the poor, they are very kind indeed; but it is a stupid cant of the day to claim, for all the poor, virtues which are not confined to any one class, thank God! Sometimes the poor are cruel, and Mary Horton's landlady happened to be one of these. Then a young girl who had seen her in her illness, took compassion on her, and she was moved to a hospital. Delirium came on, and went away, and she was left there, a poor forlorn waif. She was very pretty, and she was destitute when she left the hospital.

Over this part of her life let us pass, if you please, as swiftly and gently as possible. It was very short and horrible.

Donald meanwhile knew nothing of all this. Nay, his father had not scrupled to deceive him, in such sort that he thought Mary fickle, or at any rate forgetful, and then struggled to forget himself. It would have been better for them both had the truth been known. The Captain had ventured to play Providence, but his scheme was turning out very ill. So that these two things happened on one and the same day.

Captain Grant received a commission for his son, and going to his room found the gallant officer of the future huddled up on his bed with his boots on, and with evident signs of disorder and debauch upon his countenance.

Thus far was *he* "improved" by "life" under the auspices of his prudent father.

Mary Horton left the hospital.

Thus had *her* destiny been shaped by a man not naturally unkind, but wilful and headstrong in his own conceit.

And for the Captain himself? Years seemed to have come upon him suddenly; he grew old before his time; he was weary and tired, and sorrow-stricken and worn-out.

Thus, to sum up, three people began a new life at the same time :—

Donald Grant, who sailed away to India.

Mary Horton, who once vanished into a Highland mist and vanished now into a London fog.

Captain Grant, who found his chief hope blighted, and had to console himself as best he might.

* * * * *

There is no room here to deal with particulars. You may elaborate every detail of an hour; when you have to do with years, you have to summarize, often imperfectly, often erroneously. Of the three folk with whom we are concerned, the *compte rendu* must be brief and hasty, and then we bring them again upon the scene, as another climax, another crisis may demand.

The young soldier went away. The chief sense in his heart was a desire for change; he had tried London, and it had tired him. Away in the East, after passing through the usual stage of "griffinhood," he got to take an interest in his work. The fellow would be indeed a dull one, who, in the first flush of manhood, could find himself set in authority over grave and bearded oriental gentlemen without a kind of feeling that herein, in this great trust, was involved as great a duty. Boggles, who flukes from Eton into epaulettes, may forget this thing; to young Grant, the old clan-feeling stood instead of any definite reflection on the subject. He accepted his regiment as, in some sort, his tribe, loved his work, and did it well. The number of Britons, however, who do their duty well, is, thank God, so large, that this would have done him little good *in re* promotion, though much as regards his own moral growth and development. But there came stirring times at last, and he got his chance.

He was known in his regiment as a man passionately fond of field-sports and of "the big game," also as a man who read much, also as a man who seemed to be very old for his age. He stuck to his duties, never kept aloof from whatever social fun might be going on in his "station" or "cantonment," but he was hardly popular. In honest truth, two remorses at least weighed upon him; he felt as if he had injured, disappointed, wounded his father; and as if, to sum the whole affair up quickly, he had been very fickle and shamefully feeble in his conduct towards the poor little girl whom he still loved. The look of Donald Grant was a good deal changed; the florid face had been baked by India into a ruddy brown, long moustaches curled over his lips, and there were dark circles under his eyes, and stern lines on his forehead. He did well in his profession; rose to places of trust.

Of a sudden there came upon India a dead calm, an awful silence. Throughout the land there was at once an apparent quiescence and a marvellous activity—a nervous, electrical vivacity. Men who could read the signs of the times—who could look out boldly and with clear vision towards the political horizon, saw a great cloud gathering slowly. The vague sense of an unseen danger, the mysterious foreboding of an unknown peril, filled their souls. And at last the storm burst.

Some day or another a poet-historian will write a grand record of English resistance. It was superb, it was kingly, it was worthy of a race destined to rule the earth. Little blonde ensigns charged, with their white teeth clenched, and their puny fists doubled, right into thousands; grim old bearded colonels awoke to chivalry; civilians vied with soldiers in gallant endurance, and the ladies—God bless them!—so far from troubling this free heroic spirit, breathed into it a great passion and fire. In that struggle, Donald Grant was fortunate enough to have a chance or two. His own regiment turned against him; would not take his life, but stormily marched away to help their kinsmen. He was one of the few officers whom they spared. Soon after, he reached an outlying station that was besieged by the rebels. Provisions ran short in the fort; privations and bullets removed the majority of the English leaders. Grant one day, by this time a lieutenant, saw that the only chance left, and it was desperate, lay in a sortie. On a Sunday, the chaplain, whose own physical strength was fast failing him, but whose courage never faltered, administered the Sacrament to the faithful little company who were beleaguered; on the Monday the sortie was made; and when the odds seemed heavily against the English, there was a sudden wavering in the enemy's line, and a cloud of dust far away. Later, there came a ringing cheer in the jolly, manly tone of our race; the station was saved, and Grant, with a great sword-gash on his face, heard, as he fainted, a loud cry of victory.

Then the women gathered round him, nursing. He soon recovered. In days like those, a man's superb vital force and pluck enable him to bear up against wounds very readily; he fails only when the excitement is over, and the reaction has set in. Recovering, he gained fresh honours, and when the great mutiny had been trodden under foot by Colin Campbell, he came home.

If *his* life had for many years hung heavily upon his hands, and had only become tolerable when at length a great national crisis gave him a chance, judge how the years had passed at home with Mary! After a very short and terrible period, she had found friends, and worked from that time in many ways—all hard enough, but all honest. By degrees she drifted towards the theatre. She was very handsome, though with a beauty that would rather awe than attract. She had admirers, of course, but she was quite indifferent to their admiration. Nay, she had suffered so horribly, that her temper had grown fierce and resentful; she could not look upon her life with resignation, she regarded it with intense and disdainful anger, she despised herself even more than she despised others. Yet there were some of her friends to whom she was different in her bearing—and one of these was a man older than herself, one John Lane, who watched over her with a kind of canine fidelity. He was merely a violin-player in an orchestra, but he had a little money from other sources—amongst other things, from lessons. He was shrewd, kindly, a little selfish. When Mary, after many tentatives in other directions, tried the stage, John Lane saw that her ultimate success was certain. He set himself to work for her, rendered her many services, made himself necessary to her, and won, at least, her gratitude and affection. When he asked her to marry him, which at length he did, Mary was frank and honest in reply, told him of her hideous troubles, and also of the love which preceded them, owned that her heart was untouched by him in the way that a woman's should be by the man who seeks her for a wife; but, for the rest, confessed that she liked him much, was grateful to him—briefly, would marry him if, knowing all this, he still persevered. John Lane pressed his suit; they were married, very quietly, nor were they altogether unhappy. Love on his part, cordial liking and gratitude on hers, were the elements of a tolerably peaceful married life. But her heart was still hungry. John Lane was a good husband, no doubt, and she was true and good to him, but her life seemed a waste. At length, John, after infinite diplomacy, so succeeded that Mary was engaged at a leading London theatre. This engagement was to her what the Indian Mutiny was to Grant; it called forth her full capacity, gave her something about which she could be in earnest. Before long she was recognized. With her stern beauty, sombre and passionate, she swayed the hearts of her audience more potently than by winning graces and pleasant smiles, on which most of her rivals depended. As she swept across the stage, you trembled, for in her eyes there was a light which was terrible, and the voice resonant and musical though it was, could also give such point to a sneer, such hideous emphasis to a sarcasm, such rage of expression to invective, that involuntarily you shuddered, as before a woman who had some private grief, some private wrong, some misery upon which she brooded, and which tortured her very soul.

And now for the third life, for this, after all, was the saddest. Grant's father, as we said, tried to guide Grant; but who could guide Grant's father? The Captain missed his boy very much. Their relations had grown somewhat cold and embarrassing, but, when Donald was absolutely gone, the Captain's love seemed to redouble. All their awkwardness, their petty troubles, went out of the Captain's mind. He could only think of the finest

qualities of the lad, forgot the sorry way in which
Donald had yielded to London, and simply recol-
lected the Highland time. They had lived so long
together that the house was horribly lonely without
Donald. Then his letters, when they came, were
certainly affectionate; but to the father it seemed as
though they were marked by a certain restraint,
as if their very affection were hardly free and
natural, but rather a mere matter of duty. All this
pained him bitterly. What had he done? He had
kept Donald from sacrificing his prospects in life,
had saved him from a ridiculous marriage. Yes;
this was true; but at what cost? Was Donald, no
matter what his prospects, at all happy or contented?
The Captain knew that he was not; and so there
preyed upon him this double regret—that he had
lost some portion of his son's affection, and that he
had not succeeded in his plans for his son's good.
He left London now and then for Scotland; but it
was dreary and sad to tramp about with his keepers,
and without Donald. All their favourite haunts—
bridges, ledges of rock, and so forth — only reminded him of his loss. Then he grew gloomy, and
drank. By and by field-sports had no longer any
charm for him, and his life grew to be without an
object. No doubt Donald would return some time
or other, but it would not be the same Donald. He
wanted him back, and yet feared to see him. It would
be sweet to go down to the old spots with him if the
lad had not changed. Letters came frequently
enough, but they were not very long ones, nor so

cordial as those of a son should be; and the father winced as he saw that Donald was growing worldly-wise after his fashion, and that the fashion was not a good one. He had failed—obviously made a bungle of his interference. These thoughts haunted him perpetually, and he grew to be very wretched. A lonely man, getting old, too, what use was he to anybody, even to himself? He had money; but there were things which it could not buy him. "An useless old stager, sir!" would the Captain say to his few intimates.

Nor were his associates of the best kind. He disliked now those quiet English drawing-rooms to which he used to introduce Donald so proudly; the sight of that kind of domestic happiness hurt him. He saw parents who certainly could not love their children more than he, surrounded by grown-up sons who were taking their place in the world, and doing credit to their names. So was Donald, too, no doubt; he was a capital soldier, of course; all the Grants would be *that*; but he was buried in India, and the old man's heart was fierce and angry, and yet torn by a wild craving to see his son again, to live the good old life once more. How could he bear this misery? he asked himself. How could any one bear it—lonely, wretched old man! He would go no more into houses where he saw such happiness—which was given so readily to other people, denied so cruelly to him! Few people, who saw him walking quietly to his club, guessed what a furnace of passion was burning within him—with what wild cries, at night-time, he woke, shouting for Donald—or how he hated the house his son had left. Long hours he would sit in the study, brooding over this curse that had seemed to come upon him, until he could not bear to sit alone any more.

He went about amongst men to whom his nature would have been unintelligible—calm, cynical men of the world, with their affections very much under their own control. He needed excitement, and he found it where such a man was likely to seek it—at the gaming-table. He cared little for money lost or won; what he needed was the morbid emotion of the gambler. This he got; and then steadily went down-hill, drifting on to a miserable old age, losing his own self-respect, and only happy sometimes in dreams.

The most reckless excesses are not those of youth; they are those committed by men who, after living reputably for many years, break loose again.

*   *   *   *   *

Sailing homeward, Donald Grant had many bad dreams; but he never fancied that there would be any very great change in his father. The stormy life he had led had somewhat tired him. The struggle was superb while it lasted. Now that it was over, and his nerves were no longer at full tension, the chief desire of his soul was rest. He had lived at high pressure; but there is a time for all things. As he paced the deck of an evening, and watched the glory of the sunset, thoughts of the old home rushed in upon him, so that he yearned to see his father, and then to go back into Scotland with him, and wander about arm-in-arm. He had seen grander mountains than Cruachan; but he wanted now to watch the curl of the clouds around the *old* hill. Glenorchy would seem very small after the great gorges of the Himalayas, and there was the memory about it of a deep sorrow. Still he would like to gaze again at a salmon-pool, and see the mountain-ashes once more; and as for his disappointment, *that*, as he supposed, could give him no further pain. Just one twinge, perchance, like the aching of an old wound, might he suffer when he came to the spot where he parted with Mary; but it was very long ago. Doubtless she was married by this time; if not, did it greatly matter? He had gone away a boy; he was coming back a man; yet there leapt up in his heart the spirit of boyhood, eager and exultant, as he thought of the long, long days that he would pass with his father. Of course, father would be old; hardly able to do much in the way of deer-stalking. Well, perhaps that, too, was all the better. Grant bethought himself how his father used to lift him in his arms when he tired; how he took him to all the loveliest nooks about the country. Well, this would be changed now; it would be *his* turn to guide and support; and with a very tender love he thanked God that he had been spared in battle, and saved from disease, to go home to his father thus, and comfort him.

The Captain knew that his boy was coming back; but Donald had started earlier than he first intended,

and would himself bring the first news of his actual
return. The old man winced as he thought of the
meeting. He looked in the glass, saw his wrinkles;
but saw also that he had not been altered merely by
time. He grew very miserable and ashamed. That
he should have to meet his son *thus*; to be afraid of
him! It was a bad ending to a life, this. He had
made a very wretched business of it after all. He
was grey;—but venerable? What? That man
who slinks into a gambling-house, and watches the
turn of the game with eyes bloodshot and bleared,
who is almost the mockery of younger players, the
pity of a few men of his own time, you could hardly
call *him* venerable! Could he not break away from
all this, and make himself a little worthier of his
son, whose name had figured with honour in
Outram's own despatches? No; it was too late, or
else he was too feeble. Still would Donald but come,
and love him a little better than he feared, they
might go away together—away from this horrible
city that had so profaned and polluted both of them
—back to the old house. Father and son both had the
same simple plan of life; but it was all in the future.
And now, just now, until Donald came, the Captain
could not do much by himself. Besides—and this
was the dreariest thought, this it was which brought
tears, childish tears, to his eyes—Donald might be
shocked at his utter wreck—might find it hard to
love him in the old way. The poor man's nerve was
gone; and there was only one means now by
which he could ever rouse himself to action—even

to action that did but bring nearer the bad, bad End.

As Donald hurried on—finding steam itself slow, so great grew his impatience—a strange morbid restlessness possessed him—a nervous irritability. He was petulant with his own servants, moody and reserved with his fellow-passengers. There is little time wasted by the Overland route; but the hours seemed to grow horribly long. He could do nothing to get on faster; and this sense of impotence, absurd though he felt it to be, annoyed him. He slept little, and never woke refreshed. Nay, to the doctors it seemed as though he were lashing himself into a state of fever; and one man cautioned him, but got scanty thanks for the warning.

Marseilles at last; and the train thundered along across France too slowly for his haste. His overwrought brain seemed to pant and throb with every beat of the engines; and with his head thrust out of the window, facing the rush of wind, he could have shouted to the very stokers, and sworn at them for making no more speed.

And now, on a foggy day, he crossed the Channel, peering out through the mist for the first English light; and then again the train thundered, and again his brain panted and throbbed.

It was a dull November evening when he reached London, and the place seemed hatefully squalid to him as he drove home to his father's house. Any noise seemed to drive him mad; the very rattle of his cab-wheels worried him.

The Captain was not at home. It was uncertain when he would return, the servants said. He might be late; he was sometimes late. Wouldn't the gentleman call again? Oh! it was Mr. Donald? Yes; would Mr. Donald wait?

It was hard to have hurried as he had, and get *this* for his welcome; but a real disappointment troubled him less than his merely fantastic miseries. Nay, now that he had got home, and the life of his dreams could not be many hours from him, he was almost pleased that a little time longer was left.

He walked out into the streets, laughing at himself. How ridiculous had been his impatience! What a cross-grained, evil-tempered wretch he had been on the journey! Well, it was all right now; he had but to kill a few hours.

His father might be late? Then Donald thought of the old man again; fancied him at his club, smoking his honest cigar with some other old Indians; talking about himself very likely; a grey-haired man, but handsome still, and courtly; proud of his son, too. What a life they would have!

How to pass the time? He would not hunt for his father; he did not want strangers at that meeting.

He strolled into a theatre, the first he passed; and for a time the figures on the stage were mere puppets, scarcely visible, indeed, for his *own* drama was what he thought about, as he sat there indolently, with half-shut eyes, and twitched now and then his yellow beard, and played with his long mustaches idly.

But at length a sudden burst of applause roused him from his reverie. The great actress of the night entered. A strange, wild thrill went through him like a sword-thrust, as he saw her; the look of the man changed at once as he rose in his stall, erect and eager, careless of the cry to sit down, and waited until she spoke. It was *her* voice, richer and fuller, but *hers*; and then, as with a superb gesture she turned, she saw him; and, with a spasm, she seemed for just one second to reel upon the stage as though she would fall, then, conquering her pain by her courage, magnificently declaimed. But she never looked that way again all night, and when Lane carried her home, she fell with a pitiful moan upon the floor, and would not rise. Could she but faint;—no; consciousness, fiery, intense, never left her for a moment.

The whole love of Donald's heart had yearned towards her again; the passion long suppressed had rebelled and triumphed. And in the hour when it arose, he learnt that it was hopeless—that Mary was married.

How brave she was! how gloriously she had borne herself in that fierce momentary ordeal!

Then there came a great bitterness in Grant's soul—a recollection almost angry of their old love—almost wrathful of his father's conduct. He shuddered at his own evil thoughts; but he could not yet go home—not yet for a little while.

Moodily he walked about the streets. He had not known what a place that love of his yet held in his heart. Still there was much left to live for; and solemnly he blessed his father, to whom he would say no word that should arouse the recollection of their one dispute.

He turned homewards; and then came the pang, then came the culminating agony. For, as he approached the house, he passed an old man who was staggering unsteadily; and as he turned aside to avoid him, their eyes met.

* * * * *

They had wept together. Their love had survived sorrow—even shame.

Donald was in bed, stupid and insensible, neither waking nor asleep.

The old man sat alone in The Study. His head rested between his hands; but when he raised it a little, there was on it an awful look of wistful sorrow, and a strange, pitiful bewilderment. His nerves were shattered—nerves? why his very heart was crushed.

He tried to plot and think; but the blood rushed to his temples, and his head seemed as though it would burst. After a time he pulled his writing-case towards him. His hand shook, for many reasons; but with his faltering fingers he scrawled a few lines, idly repeating words:—

"My DEAR, DEAR BOY,—After a little while I shall be better, and we will see each other again, and live very happily, but I cannot face you for a day or two."

How the dull pain grew!

"But not yet, Donald, dear. Do not blame me when you read this, but to-night I am going away."

The pain was worse. He must bathe his temples before he could end the letter. He rose from his chair, and then fell heavily forward on the table, muttering "Donald" still, as the blood trickled to the desk, staining it, and then he did not mutter any more.

"To-night I am going away," he had written, and now indeed he had gone.

* * * * *

THREE KEYS ON A SMALL RING OF THEIR OWN.

THREE KEYS ON A SMALL RING OF THEIR OWN.

CHAPTER I.

THE KEY OF THE DRESSING-ROOM.

When Mr. Everest announced one morning, with as grave a face as he could put on for the occasion, that Aunt Rachel had decided to come and live at Riverside, a very serious discussion ensued. They had all expected it for some time past, and though Edith Everest entirely agreed with her father in the course he had thought fit to adopt, she, quite as much as her little sister Mabel, secretly hoped that the evil day would somehow or other be averted.

And indeed it was a "horrid shame," as Mabel expressed it, to have to introduce an element of discord into that peaceable and unusually happy family circle. Mrs. Everest had died soon after the birth of Mabel, the youngest girl, and ever since then the father and his two daughters had lived together more like brothers and sisters than anything else. The house in which they resided was charmingly situated in the heart of the very loveliest part of the Thames scenery, and Mr. Everest invariably found it no easy task to tear his pretty nymphs away from their river-home, just when the water-lilies were beginning to unfold themselves, and the forget-me-nots to bloom, in order to respond to the authoritative summons of the fashionable world, and see the roses on their cheeks fade under the influences of glare and gas-light, late hours, and London ball-rooms.

Mr. Everest was a very wealthy London merchant, and though of course he could have lived on a far grander scale than he did at Mapledurham, he was not at all anxious to take any step which his children would have objected to; and, indeed, would himself have thought it a great hardship to be compelled to leave the dear old home.

Each year slipped away merrily enough, but there was one fact which seemed entirely to have been passed over or forgotten at Riverside. Edith Everest was no longer a child, but had suddenly bloomed into a tall, and singularly handsome young woman. No wonder, then, that Aunt Rachel shuddered when she heard that her beautiful niece was "running about wild" in the country, and suddenly became painfully alive to the fact that there was no one at hand to form the poor child's character, as she called it, or to guide her safely through the intricate paths which wind round hat great institution styled "Vanity Fair."

Mrs. Richardson, or Aunt Rachel, was a widow,

of about five or six and fifty, and a very great person in her own estimation. She was certainly of the world worldly, and though of good, but certainly by no means distinguished family, set up a god called Aristocracy, and worshipped it, and was continually parading her hackneyed platitudes about birth, family, and gentle blood. Her manner no one could find fault with, and her address was very ladylike though perhaps rather over-studied, and she had the good sense so to control her temper, which was not of the sweetest, as to reserve the worst of it entirely for those immediately and closely connected with her. On the death of her husband she came into a very large property, both in land and money, of which last article she certainly was not prodigal; for, indeed, there were people unkind enough to declare that the worthy lady was not only a sparing woman, but what they could not help calling a close-fisted one. The generous offer, then, of her services in Edith Everest's behalf was not so disinterested as it might have appeared at first sight, since on being installed in her brother's comfortable mansion in Hyde Park Gardens, during the approaching season, it was quite possible both to forget and forego the cares and expense of her own establishment at Rutland Gate.

Be that as it may, though both Mr. Everest and Edith were perfectly aware that Aunt Rachel was a necessary evil, they determined to do their best to make everything smooth for her when she arrived, and made up their minds to enjoy thoroughly the last little bit of peace and quiet that was left them at Riverside, before the time came for their departure for town, when Aunt Rachel was really to arrive, and Edith was to be introduced into the very best society, and Mabel was to go through a course of governesses and fashionable masters.

That last happy month passed too quickly for all of them, and long before it was wanted came the day which had been fixed for their departure.

Mabel took her last peep at the swan's-nest hidden by the rushes in the stream, Edith made her last sketch of the pretty house, now almost lost among the fresh green trees, and they all walked for the last time in the woods newly-carpeted with primroses, and sweet with the early violets. And then came the sound of carriage-wheels and the lumbering of trunks, and an inevitable farewell to dear old Riverside!

It was some consolation to them all that Aunt Rachel altered her plans so far as coming down into the country was concerned; but, when the Everests arrived at Hyde Park Gardens, they found her fully installed, and she received them most graciously. Seeing that Edith Everest was a very lovable as well as an unusually beautiful girl, and when to these charms was added the fact that she was likely to be a very rich heiress, it may reasonably cause some surprise that she found herself, at the age of twenty, with her heart still in her own possession. Strange to say, there had, really, been no lovers; but then Edith was not quite like the ordinary run of young ladies, who, when similarly gifted, seldom conduct themselves in as sensible a manner. To begin with, she despised anything like a flirtation, and, what is more, showed as decidedly as her sweet and gentle nature would permit, how much she despised it to those who ever attempted this dangerous, but at the same time very enjoyable amusement. It was quite evident that love with her would be a great absorbing passion, and it was equally certain that she could never teach herself to love. Those who knew her best felt that her heart, when once gained, would be a prize almost beyond all price.

Besides, she was too happy with her father and sister to think of tearing herself away from them, and too contented with her present position to dream of throwing herself in love's way. There was a cousin certainly, one Arthur Oldham, of whom she was excessively fond. It would have been a difficult matter to define the kind of love she felt for him. It was somehow stronger than a sister's love, but it seemed to stop short of the actual reality. They had been brought up together ever since they were children, and many were the delightful days they spent together when Arthur was a little manly fellow, glowing with all the pride and gentlemanliness of a full-blown public-school boy, and Edith revelling in the glories of short-frocks and mischief. And after that Arthur went to Oxford, and insisted upon spending nearly all the "vac" at Riverside; and then the time slipped away again, and he found himself in chambers at the Temple, pretending to read hard at law, but really writing leading articles and papers for magazines, and constantly running away from Saturday to Monday to the house down by the river, where he always received the warmest of welcomes, till he came to be considered quite a member of the family. In fact he was

> "Ever called away
> By one low voice to one dear neighbourhood;
> And often, in his walks with Edith, claimed
> A distant kinship to the gracious blood,
> That shook the heart of Edith hearing him."

There was no doubt whatever about his love for Edith Everest, and he very frequently reflected that he was not altogether behaving well in putting himself so far in a false position, and in continually plunging further and further into the wood; but the poor fellow could not help it. He knew perfectly well that he ought to have gone abroad, and taught himself to forget all about the girl that was "so near and yet so far" from him. But then, like many of us, he had not the moral courage to carry his honest thoughts into execution; and

> "So they wander'd, hour by hour,
> Gather'd the blossom that rebloom'd, and drank
> The magic cup that filled itself anew."

Edith Everest had not been in London six weeks before she was really in love. Her father was naturally rather proud of his beautiful daughter, and he used to be very fond of taking a stroll after church on Sunday afternoons, "just to see the fine folks in the park." Edith invariably went with him. It was a duty-walk at first with her, as she never hesitated to say that she strongly objected to the absurd custom, as she used to call it, of parading up and down to look and be looked at. It was not long, however, before she looked forward to those Sunday walks with feverish excitement. Times had changed with her, the whole course and purpose of her life was somehow altered, and all through the day there was one face that haunted her.

Why was it that her heart beat so quickly, and that her hand almost trembled in her father's arm, on one of these eventful Sundays? There had been no bow, no recognition; no one had spoken to her; but still she knew as well as possible there was one face in the crowd she had seen before, and more than that, she felt that its influence was very great indeed. Again their eyes met, again a thrill of excitement seemed to rush through all her veins, and again she moved on with the crowd, and all seemed darkness. Now she remembered it all.

She had been staying in Gloucestershire the year before, and during her visit had taken the well-known trip from Bristol to Chepstow, and so along the "babbling Wye" to lovely Tintern Abbey, not forgetting a peep from the Windcliffe, from which may be seen one of the loveliest views in all England.

The boat was full of excursionists of course, and everybody, as very often happens, was discussing everybody else. The usual newly-married couple was soon singled out, and heartlessly pulled to bits; and so was the old snob from London, loud of voice, and full, as to his pockets, with brandy-flasks and bank-notes. The three young men, quietly smoking short pipes on the paddle-box, were evidently on a walking tour. The tallest and the handsomest of the three interested Edith singularly. He laughed so loud, and was so full of fun, and at the same time seemed to talk so well and sensibly—for she could not help hearing every word that was said—that she took to him at once; and somehow or other, when there was a lull in the conversation, Edith's eyes wandered away from the scenery, and invariably met his, which were constantly fixed on her. Wherever they went they met that day—on the steps of the hotel at Chepstow—in the little arbour on the topmost height of the Windcliffe—amidst the ruins of Tintern Abbey. They seemed to be drawn together by a kind of fate, and the last time they came across one another they could not possibly help smiling. Of course they never spoke, and of course, when evening came on, they were many miles apart.

The same face that haunted Edith all that day, now seemed to pursue her wherever she went in London.

At last they met at a public ball in London, and were very soon introduced to one another. They had a good laugh over what they chose to call quite a romantic adventure, and soon became firm friends. They danced repeatedly together that evening, and talked long and earnestly about the chance of meeting again, and even made arrangements about reserved waltzes and special quadrilles in case they did.

"What a singularly handsome and gentlemanly man Lord Roseworth is," said Aunt Rachel, as they drove home from the ball in the early hours of the morning.

"And who might he be?" replied Edith, knowing well her aunt's particular hobby about well-bred people, and imagining she had been whiling away the time in the enjoyment of a quiet tête-à-tête with some aristocratic old beau.

"Why surely, my dear child, you know who that young man was with whom you were dancing so repeatedly, and whose conversation seemed to please you vastly."

"Is his name Lord Roseworth—a real live lord? You don't say so. I never knew that the nobility could be half so entertaining. He is a most delightful man; one of the nicest men, in fact, I have ever met."

Aunt Rachel was delighted. Here was an opportunity. What a chance to try her hand at match-making, a match indeed that would do her such infinite credit. She determined she would try.

Edith guessed the meaning of all the unusual affection on separating for the night, and now for the first time understood why she had been allowed to "make herself conspicuous with" Lord Roseworth that evening. She determined, however, to flatter the good lady's vanity so far as to withhold from her all about the Tintern Abbey meeting, in order to make her believe that she was ready to be guided by her aunt's sound advice.

After that Edith Everest and Lord Roseworth met constantly, and Aunt Rachel helped on the love-making wonderfully.

Little Mabel Everest was woke up very early one sunny summer morning by somebody entering her room. Her sister stood at the foot of the bed looking very lovely, but evidently just returned from a ball, as her tumbled dress and faded flowers showed. In a few moments the two sisters were clasped in one another's arms, and both were shedding tears. Little Mabel's tears sprung from her heart, and were very bitter; but Edith's were tears of joy. Edith Everest and Lord Roseworth were engaged to be married!

About this time everybody noticed how ill Mr. Everest was looking, and remarked that he seemed vexed and anxious. He was evidently working too hard, and his daughters used to protest against the late hours in the city, and declared it was high time for him to give up work, and live quietly at home and enjoy himself. If there was one thing he disliked talking about more than another, it was his daughter's engagement.

Both the young people were anxious that some

understanding should be come to on the matter, for Mr. Everest had really never formally given his consent. Lord Roseworth's appeals had been put off from time to time, and Aunt Rachel's advice had been quietly resisted. Edith was not at all anxious to force the matter on her father, as she was well aware it seemed a painful subject to him. He did not like the idea of parting with her she thought, and she loved him for it more than ever.

At last, however, Lord Roseworth persuaded her to try what her influence would do; so one morning she followed her father after breakfast into the study. For the first time in their life, the father and daughter seemed constrained. Mr. Everest walked about the room uneasily, and talked about the most indifferent subjects; while Edith stood by the fire-place nervously playing with her watch-chain. At last she spoke out boldly, and he was obliged to listen. After the affair had been quietly discussed some little time, Edith said, quietly—

"Tell me, my dear father, your real opinion about the matter; you know I will be guided by you in everything. Have you any very serious objection?"

"Not in the least, my child, not in the least!"

And then he came quite close to her, and, when he had kissed her, he said—

"It is no use beating about the bush. We have never hid any secrets from one another—have we, my child? You must know everything one day or other, so it may just as well be known at once."

Edith shuddered at these words, and looked earnestly at her father as he went on.

"It has nothing whatever to do with Lord Roseworth. He is an excellent fellow in his way, and would, I trust, make you a good husband. But do you think, my child, he would care to marry a girl without a penny? He thinks you are an heiress, Edith, and so you were. I have ruined you as well as myself!"

"Ruined, father, absolutely ruined! you can't mean that!"

"Yes, Edith, it is only too true; everything has turned out badly with me lately. I thought to make matters better by speculating madly, but now I have lost nearly everything. If I were young and active as I once was, I should not care so much; but these last few years have aged me wonderfully, and I am almost past work. But God's will be done, my darling, God's will be done!"

Great, big tears rolled down the poor man's face as he spoke thus, and looked imploringly at his daughter.

She bore up wonderfully, and tried to comfort him, and persuade him that all, perhaps, might be well.

"You were always my right hand, Edith, and I am sure you will bear with me now. Besides, you have courage, and will always make your way.

My heart sinks, though, when I think of the misery I have brought on poor Mabel."

"Don't fret yourself about Mabel, father, we will take care of her; and, when she is old enough, I'll find her a husband, and make her as happy as I shall be."

"You will take care of her? A husband—happy!" murmured the old man.

"Yes. Why, of course, matters are not nearly so black as they look. Lord Roseworth has quite enough for us all to live upon for a time, and I am sure his kind, generous heart would be the first to feel for us."

"My poor child—my poor, poor child!" sobbed Mr. Everest. He could say no more, but he thought of the pain and sorrow that might be in store for this noble girl, and moaned again in anguish at the misery he had caused.

"Promise me one thing, Edith," said her father before they parted. "Do not breathe a word of all this just yet. Nothing is at all definitely settled, but I shall receive a letter in a few days which will decide our fate. Meanwhile, we will all go down to Riverside for a week, and try and forget all about the misery and sorrow that seems threatening in the distance. Write one line to Arthur Oldham, who has just returned from Italy, and ask him to come down to us as usual on Saturday, if you don't mind; and if you can possibly contrive to exist without seeing Lord Roseworth for a week, you will oblige me excessively. Send him a note, however, to say that his anxiety will soon be relieved. The letter must come by the end of the week, and that will settle everything."

Accordingly, they all went down to Riverside, and Arthur Oldham came on the Saturday.

He noticed the fretful anxiety of Mr. Everest, and his heart bled at the sight of Edith's pale, care-worn face. He knew nothing of what had passed between the father and daughter, and there had been no time for him to hear of Edith's engagement; but he had heard something very serious at Marseilles, and felt he had a duty to perform.

Arthur and Edith walked together in the woods on the Sunday evening, and he was determined, cost what it might, to tell her all.

"I have something most important to tell you," said he, "something which I am sure you ought to know; but I never really felt such a difficulty in speaking to you as I do now."

"Nonsense, Arthur," said his cousin, "we must never have any secrets; and I somehow fancy the day is not very far distant when I shall want your serious assistance."

"The fact is," said Arthur, "I heard, from the very best authority at Marseilles, that your father's affairs were in a terrible condition, and that the failure of his house was all but imminent."

Edith become deadly pale, and, turning away, said, "It can't be true!"

"Let us hope and pray that it is not," said Arthur. "At any rate, I felt that you, of all others, ought to know this; and there is another thing which you ought and which you must know, Edith, no matter what fate is in store for both of us — I love you with all my heart and soul, and would work for you to the last day of my life."

Edith removed from his arm the hand, which he was clasping passionately, and said to him almost fiercely,

"You have no right to talk to me like this. I am engaged!"

Poor Arthur could hardly keep back his tears.

He struggled bravely to explain that he knew nothing of what had passed while he was away, and to apologize for his hastiness, but he utterly broke down, and leaving his cousin as soon as he could,

"Had his dark hour unseen, and rose and past,
Bearing a life-long hunger in his heart."

But Arthur Oldham went up to London that night with Edith's, as well as Mabel's kisses fresh on his lips. They were both his sisters now.

And so they were all back again at pleasant Riverside; but somehow or other a dark cloud seemed to be hanging over the once merry little family. No one thought of alluding to the difference, but it was very evident that both father and daughters felt that something was amiss. Mabel, who was of course entirely ignorant of the real cause of the melancholy fit, which seemed so entirely to have taken possession of her father and sister, tried to laugh it all off, and to teaze the refractory ones into happiness again. But Edith resisted all her pretty sister's entreaties to accompany her in the little boat along the back-water in search of water-lilies and forget-me-nots for the drawing-room table, and Mr. Everest could not be persuaded to shake off his gloominess, and ramble with Mabel in the woods to hunt out new specimens for her fern-case.

On the Friday evening after Arthur Oldham had left, a letter arrived for Mr. Everest, and Edith contrived to get her father alone before going to bed, in order to ask him about its contents.

"Well, nothing is absolutely settled, my darling, after all," said he; "but it will be necessary for me to go up to London by the very first train. Just tell the servants to call me by six o'clock, and even earlier if possible. I shall have a good deal of work to do before starting. Don't you think of getting up in the morning, as they will get me my breakfast, and I don't intend to rob you of any of the sleep which will do you so much good after all this worry."

"It is not very likely I shall let you leave us in that miserable way, you silly man," said Edith, kissing her father, affectionately. "I shall get up and see after you of course. At any rate try and get this horrid business over as quickly as you can, and mind and come back to-morrow evening, and let me know how you have sped."

Mr. Everest turned away his head and sighed

bitterly, but then seeming to recollect himself, he moved to his daughter again, saying,

"Well, good-bye, and God bless you, my very darling child!"

"Not good-bye, not good-bye," replied Mabel through her tears.

The tears were rolling fast down the poor old man's cheeks. Again and again he pressed his daughter to his heart and covered her face with kisses.

And so they parted for the night.

In the dull haze of the early morning Edith Everest was awakened by a dull heavy knocking, which seemed to echo through the house. She had passed a miserable, restless night, and had lain awake for hours, fearful lest she should by chance oversleep herself, and anxious about the events of the last few weeks. Nature, however, at last would have her way, and towards morning Edith fell into a deep sleep.

At first the knocking was somehow mixed up with her dream, and though she evidently heard it, she was not conscious enough to be really disturbed. At last a long, piercing, awful shriek rang through the half empty house. And then the poor girl sat up terrified in her bed.

The shriek was still echoing in her ears as she began to collect her thoughts. All at once a terrible suspicion flashed across her, and it was the work of a moment to wrap a shawl hurriedly round her shoulders and to hasten down-stairs.

Outside her father's dressing-room door stood the servant who had been appointed to call him, wringing her hands and moaning loudly.

"Oh, Miss Edith, for Heaven's sake don't go in there, something terrible must have happened to master. He is lying on the ground and won't speak."

Edith, pale as death and speechless, hurried past the servant and flew into the room. A faint sickly smell seemed to pervade the apartment, and as she entered, her foot struck upon something which rolled away under the wardrobe. Nerving herself to the uttermost she waved away a whole crowd of servants that were hurrying into the room. And then she shut the door, and was alone with her dead father!

The first thing she did was to secure that suspicious something which had rolled away. It was a little phial. She next stooped to kiss the lips which but a few hours before had whispered, "God bless you," in her ears! But the faint sickly smell was overpowering her, and with difficulty she reached the door, round which the whole household were now gathered.

"Your master has died suddenly," she murmured. "It must have been heart disease!"

And then she turned round and locked the door.

This done she went slowly back to her own room. But her nerves would stand no more. Directly she had thrown herself on her bed she fainted away, with the key of the dressing-room tightly clasped in her hand!

CHAPTER II.

THE KEY OF THE STORE-ROOM.

The next few weeks passed away wearily enough. It is useless to describe the sorrow into which the whole family was plunged. Mabel at first was hysterical with grief, and almost refused comfort from her sister. She used to lie awake for hours at night weeping as if her poor little heart would break, and persisting that her father could not be dead, and that she must see him again or she would herself die. Edith behaved like the grand heroine that she was. She knew that everything now devolved upon her, and her alone, and so she battled with her scalding tears. There is no grief so bitter as that which is not allowed to exhaust itself by weeping. But still without a murmur Edith Everest, whose young heart bled, bore up against the awful blow which fate had levelled at her and at them all. There was just one bright spark of hope which shone for her in all the bitterness of her despair. Now, if ever, was needed the comfort of that love which so enthralled her, now was the time to test the affection which she felt she had secured, and which she valued, oh how deeply!

But weeks passed away and yet Lord Roseworth never came.

The news of Mr. Everest's failure and sudden death spread like wild-fire. Every one had something or other to say about them, and various were the rumours and absurd the gossip to which they both gave rise. Friends, at least those who chose to style themselves so, kindly bestowed a word of pity on the "pretty penniless orphans," as they were called; but the whole affair was involved in too much mystery to allow them to alternate condescension with civility.

After the funeral, Edith and Mabel came up to London until Mr. Everest's affairs were finally settled, and the house in Hyde Park Gardens sold. Arthur Oldham was more than a brother to the poor girls in the terrible time that ensued, but Lord Roseworth studiously avoided the house in which he knew as well as possible Edith Everest was residing.

Eventually it was settled that Mabel should go to a boarding school at Brighton, and that Edith should accompany her Aunt Rachel to Moat Grange in Gloucestershire, whither that worthy lady was now compelled to retire, since there were now no loaves and fishes to live on elsewhere. She made a great parade about the disinterestedness of her conduct in taking compassion on the child of the man who had never shown her anything but true kindness, and continually expressed her hopes that her extraordinary civility would be appreciated.

Aunt Rachel was quite unaware of the point to which matters had come between Edith and Lord Roseworth, or perhaps she would have looked at her niece's indifference to all her proposals in a different light.

Edith herself soon began to have misgivings, but

she had too noble a heart to think him false. He might have heard nothing after all; it was possible he might have gone abroad and was still perhaps anxiously expecting Mr. Everest's answer, careful all the time not to push the matter further himself, according to Edith's express wish.

Still Edith kept her secret, and the day for their departure for Moat Grange was absolutely fixed.

The day before they started two letters were put into Edith's hand, as she was packing away all her little treasures before commencing her new life, the thought of which made her absolutely shudder. Mabel had gone away to school and all her happiness seemed gradually to be fading away.

She brightened up at the sight of the letters, the handwriting on both of which she knew perfectly. She thought she would keep the best till the last. She sighed just a little as she opened the first letter, which was from her cousin Arthur Oldham, for she felt somehow that she knew its contents beforehand. It ran as follows :—

MY VERY DEAREST EDITH,

I feel that I am a dreadful coward, and am perfectly aware that I run the risk of incurring you displeasure by reverting to a subject which has ever been uppermost in my mind, although *you* may this time have entirely forgotten it. After what passed one dreary Sunday evening in the woods at Riverside, I have no right to pester you with renewals of that love which you must know I have felt for you all through my life. Still you are going away; not, indeed, to a home in which you are likely to have much comfort, for I feel that you, too, dread the future which is opening for you. You told me once you were engaged. From that hour I ceased to dream that you could ever be more to me than you are at present. To cease to love you was of course impossible. From that hour to this I have refrained from asking any questions whatever, and should have felt that it was clearly my duty, under the circumstances, to refrain from seeing you as much as possible. In your great sorrow I saw that there was no one at hand to render you the assistance that at such a terrible time of course you needed. I came, Edith, for the sake of your dear father who is gone, and still I loved you in all the fulness of my heart. But that is all over now—and still you are going away. Once more I tell you I have asked no questions; once more I repeat is it impossible for you to stay? This, of course, must be my last appeal. It would be an impertinence to pester you any further. You know your own heart best, and I know it well enough to feel that with you it would be simply impossible to pretend to love. And now, Edith dearest, I have done. Your decision cannot fail to be honest. If it is fatal to me, why then I must fight with my grief as you have done, and content myself with watching, as tenderly as I can, over the interests of one whom I am doomed to love to the end.—Yours ever,

A. O.

"Poor, dear boy!" she murmured when she had read his letter. "Poor, dear boy!"

And she then turned to the other letter, and eagerly breaking the seal, read :—

My dear Miss Everest,

I am afraid you will have thought me terribly wanting in politeness, in not having come near you all this long time. But the fact is, my people persuaded me after all that has passed, to keep away at least till this terrible business had blown over. Believe me, I have felt for you in all your troubles, and can but trust that by this time most of them have passed away. I am sorry to say I am off for a long tour on the Continent, and I do not see any chance of catching a glimpse of you before I depart. Who knows when and under what circumstances we may meet again. Perhaps fate may be propitious, and all will yet be well. I trust it may. Meanwhile I can but say, *au revoir*. Good-bye is a dreary word.

Yours very affectionately,

R.

Before she had got to the end of this heartless letter, the colour mounted to Edith's cheeks. Directly she finished it, she threw it on the table in disgust. "And this is the man I have loved!" she said to herself.

In one moment the fire which had burned

so fiercely in the young girl's heart, and which had been part of her very existence all through her trouble, died suddenly out. And then she began to despise herself for her credulity.

"Why did he write at all?" she said, crumpling the letter in her hand; "I might have comforted myself with the hope that some mistake existed. But now I know too well the worthlessness of the man, and am forced into the degradation of acknowledging that I can smart under his cowardly insults."

Edith's first impulse was to tear this letter into a thousand atoms, but she reflected, and thrusting them both into her bosom, covered her face with her hands, and sobbed bitterly.

In this position she remained for hours, tormenting herself with reflecting on all the happiness of the life which was now quite gone, and pondering over the dreariness of the existence which was just about to commence.

Before she went to bed that night, she made a silent vow, and she prayed long and earnestly that she might have the strength to keep it!

Aunt Rachel had a double object in offering a home to Edith Everest on the death of her father. In the first place, she liked to flatter herself into the belief that the world would think well of her for so doing, and that she would gain a reputation for being a good, kind, charitable woman; and then again she was perfectly aware of her niece's great attractions, and reflected that her beauty might, in one way or other, do credit to the family of which, as may be guessed, Aunt Rachel was uncommonly proud. Besides, Edith, according to her aunt's mode of reckoning, would not altogether, taking the bad with the good, be a worthless investment, since she inherited, through her mother, a decent little income, which would be quite sufficient to prevent any vast amount of difference in the cost of the establishment at Moat Grange. In this last matter, however, Aunt Rachel reckoned without her host. Mr. Everest's affairs at the time of his death were, of course, in very great confusion, and Edith knew enough about business to guess that many people would be great losers by the failure. Accordingly she gave directions to her father's solicitor, to appropriate her little share of her mother's fortune for the benefit of her father's creditors. This only came to Aunt Rachel's ears some little time after they were settled at the lonely house in Gloucestershire, and by no means tended to soften matters between herself and her niece, whom she discovered in a very short time to be a girl of determined spirit, and not at all inclined to submit quietly to any offensive treatment. The fact was that Aunt Rachel did not understand Edith's peculiar character in the least, and never was she more mistaken than when she tried to subdue the girl's proud spirit. Edith was never violent, and had the great gift of controlling her temper under any amount of provocation. She was not long, however, before she showed her aunt who was likely to be victorious in the end, if she commenced a series of pitched battles. It happened as follows.

During her father's lifetime Edith had, of course, been stinted in nothing. She had been accustomed to employ the best tradesmen, who naturally were in the habit of charging the best possible prices for their goods. This was of very little consequence to Mr. Everest, who had the credit of being a wealthy man, and it was always his particular whim to see his handsome daughter well dressed. With regard to her millinery he used even to encourage a little extravagance.

It was impossible for Edith to foresee at the time of her father's death the extent of the confusion in which his affairs were thrown. Young girls don't know very much about money matters. It was necessary, of course, for her to procure mourning before she accompanied her aunt to Moat Grange, so, not thinking at the time of her altered position, she procured all that was necessary of the same tradespeople that she had been in the habit of employing. Before she left London, as has been mentioned before, she gave full directions for the appropriation of all her little private store of money for the liquidation of her father's debts. She entirely forgot all about her own. The bills arrived in due course, and poor Edith at the time was totally unable to pay them. They travelled after her to Moat Grange, and eventually got into the hands of Aunt Rachel.

Edith happened one morning to come into the little sanctum in which her aunt after breakfast used to have a long confabulation with her housekeeper, very soon after the unhappy bills had been sent to Moat Grange.

Aunt Rachel, as may readily be guessed, was not in an enviable frame of mind. She got up hurriedly from her seat directly Edith entered, and thrusting all the documents into her niece's hand, said in a sharp tone,

"What on earth is the meaning of all this, Edith?"

Edith was quite taken aback by her aunt's disagreeable manner, and before taking the papers, looked her full in the face, as if astonished.

"Surely you understand me, my dear. Just explain."

"I don't really see what I have got to explain," said Edith; "the bills speak for themselves. They are for my mourning, which you know I was obliged to get."

"Obliged to get, yes, of course it was necessary; I don't doubt that in the least, but surely there was no reason for you to be so ridiculously extravagant."

Edith winced, but held her tongue.

Aunt Rachel snatched the bills out of her niece's hands, and turning to the housekeeper, was proceeding to make comments on several of what she called preposterous charges, and actually asked her if she did not agree with her that Miss Everest was not in a position to "deck herself out in absurd finery."

Edith blushed scarlet, but she checked the burst of indignation which started to her tongue, and saying, "Aunt Rachel, I have no right to dictate to you the manner in which a lady is usually treated, but I will not be insulted before your servants," quietly left the room.

"And this is the treatment I am to expect, and this is the house in which I am to pass my life," thought she, as she went up-stairs to her own room. And then she thought of Lord Roseworth, and what might have been, and bit her lips to prevent the bitter exclamation which was rising to them.

When she got to her own room, in which she had a favourite seat at the window commanding a lovely view, at which she was never tired of gazing, she passed by a large glass, and happening to catch a glance of her own face, stopped suddenly before the mirror.

Great, big tears were rolling down her cheeks, and she dashed them impatiently away. "Only twenty-three," she said to herself, "and there is not a day which does not bring with it these miserable tears. Will there never be an end?"

And then she threw open the window, and allowed the soft wind to play upon her burning face. She thought of the Riverside days, and of her poor dead father, and how he would grieve to see her now, and grieve more than ever to hear the secrets of her poor, troubled heart; and then she breathed a prayer that poor innocent Mabel might be spared such suffering, and might be ignorant for ever of such real misery as she had endured during the last few months. Again, her thoughts sped on, and lighted on the one she now loved next best in the world, her cousin Arthur Oldham. He too had suffered and had borne his sorrow nobly, and she blest him for it. And then all these miserably pleasant thoughts died quite away, and once more arose before her eyes the vision of the man she had loved so fondly, but who like a miserable coward, had utterly crushed her tender loving heart. This was the bitterest thought of all, and again the cruel tears came welling to her eyes, and she sobbed as if her heart would break.

That same evening Aunt Rachel had invited some of the people in the neighbourhood to dinner. The rector of the parish was to come, and the eligible curate, a comfortable-looking solicitor from the neighbouring town, was also to be of the party, and of course the family doctor, who told such capital stories, and was invariably asked everywhere. Their wives naturally came with them, good sort of people in their way, but uncommonly fond of small talk, which, to tell the truth, was in the habit of drifting, towards the end of the evening, into foolish gossip or affectionate slander. Edith Everest had not as yet been trotted out for the inspection of these worthies. A real live lady was rather a rarity in those parts, and Aunt Rachel flattered herself that the brilliancy of the niece would indirectly shed just a ray of lustre on the aunt.

The guests had all arrived, and were on the tiptoe of expectation, to see Miss Everest, of whom they had heard so much. But she was late in coming down. The ladies of the party began to be rather nervous and fidgety about their toilette. They feared they would be eclipsed. For to tell the truth, Aunt Rachel had been unwise enough to let fall some common-place remark about "great London ladies requiring an extra amount of time in preparing for dinner." How foolish of her not to have thought for one moment about the scene in the store-room!

At last the door opened, but there was no rustling of silk. Aunt Rachel could hardly believe her eyes. The solicitor's wife looked at the rector's better half, and smiled triumphantly.

Edith appeared in a plain black merino dress, which was simply relieved by a pair of white linen cuffs, and a tiny white collar fastened with a small jet brooch. A plain jet cross suspended from her neck by a narrow piece of black velvet, was the only ornament to be seen.

Aunt Rachel rose from her seat very agitated, and after she had introduced her niece to her guests, whispered hurriedly in her ear.

"My dear Edith, what can you be thinking of? Did you not know that I had asked some people to dinner? This is hardly the way to appear, is it?"

"I am sure your friends will excuse me, dear aunt," replied Edith, in quite loud enough a tone to be heard; "at any rate, you should explain to them my dependent position, and assure them that it is not *now* possible for me to deck myself out in absurd finery."

Aunt Rachel dared not say another word, and so Edith gained her point.

If Edith Everest fell in the estimation of the ladies of the party owing to the simplicity of her attire, she certainly made up for the loss of their friendship by gaining the good opinion of every gentleman present. She was unusually brilliant that evening, and long before the gentlemen left the dinner-table, it was unanimously agreed by them that Edith was certainly one of the sweetest women they had ever met.

The solicitor, who was especially taken with the young lady's winning and agreeable manner, happened to remark in the course of the evening that he was going to London the next day, and asked Edith if she had any commissions for him, as he would willingly execute them.

Here was another trump card for Edith. It was a bold game, but she thought she might safely risk it.

"Thank you, I am sure I am excessively obliged," said Edith; "if it really is no trouble to you, I will get you to transact a little business which is rather important. I don't mind confessing I could hardly undertake it myself, not indeed that I should be afraid to do so, but simply through the fear of being cheated. The fact is, that I want to get rid of a diamond *parure* which my poor dear father gave me, but which, alas! is of no use to me now. There are some bills which I shall also have to ask you to pay for me. There is nothing in the world I hate so much as being in debt."

The good solicitor, who knew Aunt Rachel well, immediately put two and two together. The rest of the party also guessed the meaning of the sale of the diamond necklace.

Aunt Rachel felt that every one was thinking of her, and she turned away to conceal her shame.

And so Edith Everest fairly won the second trick.

It was some time after this, that Aunt Rachel's housekeeper, who was exceedingly fond of Edith, and used to confide in her all her little troubles, came one morning in great distress about a letter she had received, in which she was told that her poor old mother was dangerously ill, and was begged to lose no time in coming to London. Aunt Rachel had been consulted in the matter, and had actually stated that it was perfectly impossible for her to go. The fact was, that Aunt Rachel could hardly have existed without this housekeeper. She was a very old servant, and knew better than any one else the ways and eccentricities of her mistress. What, then, was to be done? " Would Miss Edith intercede for her? She must see her poor old mother before she died," she said, "or she would never forgive herself."

Edith promised she would do her best.

At first Aunt Rachel insisted that not another word should be said on the matter. She paid the housekeeper her wages, and she would be served. Besides, there was no one at hand who could be trusted with the keys of office. It was not fair of Edith to ask her aunt to try new hands, or to encourage a system of petty robbery.

"Well, there is only one way, I suppose, in which it can be settled," replied Edith. "Do you think you can trust me? If you will only give me a trial, I will work hard to prevent your noticing any change, and promise to try and save you any annoyance. I cannot help thinking that in such a case the poor woman ought to go to her home."

"As you are so determined about it, my dear, I suppose she must go," said Aunt Rachel, "but it will be very inconvenient to me all the same. Pay her her wages and let her go. Perhaps she will not be wanted again."

A bright thought came into Aunt Rachel's head as she said this.

Edith certainly did her very best to please her aunt. She was determined to show that she was not ungrateful for all that had been done for her, and anxious to prove that fine ladies are not above working hard when the occasion presents itself. She used to get up early in the morning, and puzzle her poor head with dreary figures, determined that in her accounts—a most important matter in this instance—she would not be found fault with.

All went well for several months, in fact so well, that Aunt Rachel, studying strict economy as usual, sent a private dismissal to the housekeeper that required wages, and determined that the unpaid attendant should always be retained on the establishment.

Some little time after the dismissal of the housekeeper, the second scene between Aunt Rachel and her niece took place.

They were again in the storeroom one morning, looking over the accounts together. Aunt Rachel was in an unusually bad temper.

All the various items in the book were carefully scrutinized, and at last one was singled out as being an instance of horrible extravagance.

"I really cannot endure this any longer," said the old lady. "I shall be ruined if you go on in this reckless manner."

"My dear aunt," replied Edith, "if you will only refer back you will see that your expenditure is not a bit more now than it was in the days of Mrs. Prebble."

"I don't want to refer back and I won't refer back. All I know is, that a great deal too much money is spent. You have had an excellent education, and you ought to make use of it now in order to save my purse. But I forgot, you are not the first of your family who has thought fit to play ducks and drakes with other people's money."

At this cruel insult, which clearly alluded to the failure of Edith's father, Edith turned pale, and trembled violently. Her voice was thick and husky as she said—

"How much, then, do you consider I owe you?"

"Owe me, indeed! It is all very well to talk of owing, but perhaps you will be so good as to tell me how you intend to pay me?"

"With my wages."

"Your wages?"

Edith looked her aunt full in the face, and replied very quietly,

"I mean exactly what I said. I have heard accidentally that you have thought fit to dismiss Mrs. Prebble, finding, no doubt, that my services were equally useful, and far less expensive. On this point, however, we must come to some understanding, and at once. I have been insulted twice, and have borne it; I will not submit a third time to a similar degradation. I have quite made up my mind what to do; I will either remain here, receiving the same salary that you formerly gave Mrs. Prebble, or will seek occupation elsewhere. Mind, in that case, I cannot undertake to spare any one's feelings. If I choose to hire myself out as a nursery-governess to those who know us both equally well, and would, I am sure, give me a trial for old time's sake; or, if my inclination leads me to set up a shop in the neighbouring town, you will only have yourself to blame. In the latter case, I can assure you I shall not conceal my name. My sister will never be ashamed of me, and hers is the only love left me now. I shall be excessively obliged if you will decide this matter before the end of the week."

So saying, she took the key of the store-room out of her pocket, and, having placed it on the table by the side of her aunt, quietly left the room.

Before the end of the week came, Edith received back the key, accompanied by a polite note, begging forgiveness, and agreeing to her stipulation.

Thus Edith gained a triumphant victory; but, for the first time, reflected that all hope of leaving Moat Grange was now cut off for ever!

It was joyful news for Edith when her aunt told her one morning that she had made arrangements for Mabel to spend her holidays at Moat Grange. Here, then, was sunlight at last. In another week she was to arrive, and was to be accompanied by Arthur Oldham, who had been specially invited to come and pass a week or so with his cousins. Aunt Rachel did not, of course, know what had occurred between Arthur and Edith.

Arthur and Mabel were always the warmest of friends, and their friendship had been stronger than ever of late, for Arthur used to run down to Brighton, and beg a holiday for Mabel, and then they would wander away and have a good talk on a subject which was equally dear to them both. Mabel soon found out the true state of the case, and resolved that she would take the earliest opportunity of pleading poor Arthur's cause with her wilful sister. The poor child's simplicity was charming.

Edith thought the week would never end; but the happy day arrived at last, and the two sisters very soon found themselves alone in their snug bedroom.

At last, when Mabel's tongue was nearly tired of talking, and after Edith had said several times that it was quite time to go to bed, the little girl put her arms lovingly round her sister's neck, and told her that she had something of very, very great importance to tell her. And then she told Edith all about Arthur's love for her, and praised him, and called him a darling fellow, and related all the conversations they had had together often and often about Edith, and how they were never tired of thinking of her shut up in the miserable old house. From this she went on, and built castles in the air, and explained how they could all live together, and shake off all misery, and be happy once more, and never separate again for ever.

Edith trembled as she listened to the little girl's passionate energy. For once she forgot all about Lord Roseworth, and thought only of her sister's comfort and Arthur's unselfish love. She had almost made up her mind; and as she thought of the bright picture Mabel had painted, she drew her closer to her heart, and covered her face with kisses.

But Mabel's nerves were all unstrung, and she burst into a flood of tears. Edith hastily drew her handkerchief from her pocket to wipe them away.

A crumpled letter and a key fell at her feet!

In one instant the bright dream vanished. Both the letter and the key told its own story; and so Arthur's cause was pleaded in vain!

CHAPTER III.

THE KEY OF THE DESK.

ARTHUR OLDHAM made but a short stay at Moat Grange. Had it not been for little Mabel's warm persuasion, he would never have gone there at all. But now he had safely conveyed thither his little cousin, there was very little occasion for him to stay on. He felt that it would not be kind to Edith to remain after everything was explained; and of course it was very wretched for him to pretend to act a part which, feeling as he did, was most unattractive. Still Edith was far happier now than she had been since her father's death. She had those near her who loved her very dearly, and who were far more precious to her than any one else in the world; but she could not in reason offer any objection to Arthur's fixed determination to leave them. He was going abroad, he said, and might be away for a very long time. He could not possibly remain in London during the approaching season, when Aunt Rachel was to come up to town again, and would of course bring Edith with her.

They had one more quiet talk together before they parted.

"I am only a brother now, you know," said Arthur, as they were taking one last turn in the garden before going in, "and I could never have any secrets which you did not share. I have found out yours, however, and I feel certain that you will not accuse me of curiosity. By the merest chance in the world I heard it all, and most certainly without asking any questions."

And then he told Edith everything he knew with regard to Lord Roseworth.

"It is quite true," said she, looking steadily on the ground as they walked along.

"I believe that he has gone away," added Arthur, "although I have heard it mentioned that he will be in London for the season."

"I hope he will."

"You do not wish me to remain in England?"

"Wish you to remain? Why, Arthur?" And then, looking sweetly into his face, she continued—

"It is because you think I am alone in the world that you would remain. God bless you, Arthur."

"I am your brother, and ought always to be watching over you."

"You are far too good to me, and treat me infinitely better than I deserve; but I will not allow you to make your life miserable because I must be for ever unhappy. Go abroad, Arthur, and forget me. My case is past all cure. I shall be far better alone."

"Then you love him still?"

Without a moment's hesitation she replied, "I love but two people in the world." After this there was a long silence.

"I will do as you wish, Edith, and go away. But I can never forget you."

"Well, perhaps, I don't quite wish that, but promise me one thing. Never hide from me where you are, and if at any time I should think it necessary to send for you, will you do your best to come back? Do promise this!"

"Is there any need to ask? If I were at the other end of the world I would return."

The next morning Arthur Oldham went away. By the time that Mabel's holidays were over, the spring was far advanced, and so it was arranged that she should stay on a little longer, in order that they might all go up to London together.

Edith rather dreaded this London visit, but still she was resolved to make herself as agreeable as possible, and try and make people believe that she was quite happy and contented. Luckily her face did not contain many traces of her recent sorrow, and she returned to London, if possible, more beautiful than ever. All the young men in London raved about Miss Everest's beauty, and her name was in a very short time in everybody's mouth. Invitations poured in, and there was hardly an evening that Aunt Rachel and Edith were not to be seen either at balls, concerts, or the opera.

Aunt Rachel's "at homes" were soon attended by the very best people in London, and at last that worthy lady began to persuade herself that Edith Everest had not, after all, been a bad investment.

One day Aunt Rachel told her niece that she intended giving a very grand dinner party, and jokingly added that it would be as well if Edith made herself additionally brilliant on this occasion, as there was every chance that one of her old "flames" would be present.

"Who do you mean?" said Edith, whose colour almost forsook her.

"Why, surely, you have not forgotten Lord Roseworth?"

Edith bit her lips, and turning away her face whispered to herself, "At last!"

"You don't answer, Edith. I had imagined I had got a delightful surprise in store for you. I do trust that the poor fellow is not too late in the field, for they say that hearing of your return to town he has hurried back from Vienna. So you see the report of your fascination has travelled a long way."

"I shall be very glad to see Lord Roseworth," replied Edith.

The evening came, and the poor girl's courage almost forsook her before entering the room. Never did Edith Everest look more lovely than she did that evening. A buzz of admiration was distinctly audible when the door opened, and she made her appearance, which quickly died away as she moved majestically down the room, and a profound silence ensued. She saw Lord Roseworth's face in a mirror directly she entered, but she was never unnerved. And then their eyes met. Lord Roseworth was evidently uncomfortable. He just raised his eyes as they shook hands, but dared not let them rest long on Edith's calm and immoveable features.

However, this coldness soon wore off, and long before the end of the evening Edith Everest and Lord Roseworth became again, or appeared to be, the best friends in the world. She sang him the songs of which he used to be so fond, discussed the places where they were likely to meet, and arranged riding parties for the park in the morning. Aunt Rachel could hardly believe her eyes, fearing from Edith's manner in the morning that all hope of bringing about the match, on which she had long set her heart, was entirely lost.

Edith's clear ringing laugh was continually heard throughout the evening, and those who had been privately informed that "poor Miss Everest had not got over her father's death, and was never likely to be the same bright girl again," hardly knew what to make of this sudden transformation.

Various were the questions asked, and the reports circulated from mouth to mouth that evening. Was there really anything between Lord Roseworth and Miss Everest before her father died? Was it true that Mrs. Richardson wanted to catch the young viscount for her niece, and intended leaving her all her money? Had Edith Everest any money of her own, and was it possible that any amount of money would remove the very strong objection that Lord Roseworth's family was known to entertain regarding his alliance with a girl whose father's death was shrouded in a great deal of mystery, which had never been properly cleared up? The two young people were very much talked about that evening, but nobody seemed clearly to have made up their minds one way or another. Lord Roseworth left Mrs. Richardson's house in high spirits. He had, of course, got private information that Mrs. Richardson would leave all her money—by no means an inconsiderable amount—to Edith, and he flattered himself that his somewhat doubtful conduct after the death of Mr. Everest had not made much impression on either Edith or her aunt.

"She's a strange girl though," thought he, as he walked home that evening. "She appeared to be the same as ever, but strongly objected to a renewal of the engagement just yet awhile. Still she gave me hope. We are certainly to meet again. I don't think I really quite understand her yet. Oh! by the by, she said the past year had been a very eventful one, and promised faithfully she would hide nothing from me, and in proof of this she slipped something into my hand, which she said she would require again when the time for an explanation came."

"What can it be?"

Lord Roseworth stopped under the first gas lamp, and took something out of his waistcoat pocket. It was carefully wrapped up in silver paper, which he unfolded. The uncertain rays from the lamp fell upon a bright object.

It was a little gold key.

"How very strange!" thought Lord Roseworth, and he had not done puzzling his brains when he arrived at his own house.

They met very frequently after this; in fact, hardly a week passed that they did not see one another two or three times. It was soon whispered about everywhere that Edith Everest and Lord Roseworth were really to be married very shortly, and Mrs. Richardson was formally congratulated on all sides on the excellent match.

Lord Roseworth never doubted for an instant that all was *en train*, and thought little more of the explanation which had been promised him. He was very proud of the conquest he had made, but at the same time did not shut his eyes to the business part of the matter. He had had a private interview with Mrs. Richardson's solicitor, which resulted in sundry other private interviews between that worthy gentleman and Mrs. Richardson herself. Some little time afterwards he was asked to call again in Parliament Street, and then a bulky parchment document was placed in his hands, and after that all anxiety ceased.

In the course of another month Arthur Oldham, who was staying at Florence, received a telegram in which he was asked to return to London as soon as he possibly could.

On the day after that on which Arthur was expected to arrive, Lord Roseworth received a note from Edith Everest, asking him to call at her aunt's house on the following day.

He readily obeyed the summons, and punctually at the appointed time drove up to Mrs. Richardson's door. He was ushered into a little private morning room in which Edith used to pass most of her time. Edith Everest was seated there alone.

After a little ordinary conversation, Edith alluded to the evening on which they had met one another again at her aunt's house, and said she was anxious to fulfil the promise she had made on that occasion.

"I had really almost forgotten it," said Lord Roseworth, gaily, "but still seeing how matters stand *now*, perhaps it will be as well for us both to understand one another."

"I hope I shan't bother you by beginning in rather a roundabout way," she said, "but the story I am going to tell you is so closely connected with the life one leads every day, that I am sure you will bear with me while I tell it. It refers to a girl with whom I was at school, the very dearest friend I ever had in the world, who confided everything in me; some of the incidents have made the strongest impression on me, I can assure you, and may account to you for some of the strangeness you may have noticed in my manner."

And then Edith Everest told Lord Roseworth the whole story of her own life, carefully concealing those facts which would clearly show him to whom she was referring. She lingered on the delights of their pleasant home at Riverside, described her father's precious love, and painted in glowing colours the devotion of Arthur Oldham. From that she went on to her miserable existence at Moat Grange, and told truly how bitter were the insults which had been heaped on her, and how they had been endured for one great object. Then came the chance of an excellent position in life, and the offer of a home by a man whom the girl despised.

Lord Roseworth, who really knew very little of the incidents of Edith's life, was completely taken off his guard.

"What a delicious romance," he answered, "and what an extraordinary girl. I really think that your strong-minded friend should be persuaded to take a tour round her native land, and lecture on the duplicity and fickleness of the rising generation."

Edith Everest started to her feet.

"Lord Roseworth," she said, triumphantly, "you insult me with these words. The story you have heard is mine. One moment more and I have done. There is no need for any more enigmas. We will now come to the stern, bitter truth; and I will ask you one more favour. I said I would hide nothing from you. The secrets of my past life are contained in that desk which lies before you. Open it, Lord Roseworth, for you have got the key. I will now ask for your advice. Here are two letters written to me by the only two men that ever spoke to me of love. Read them, Lord Roseworth, and then tell me which I am to choose?"

The letters fell idly from his hands, into which he buried his face. He could not speak.

"Your silence does you infinite credit, my lord. I see you approve my choice. Before the end of the year I shall be Arthur Oldham's wife!"

* * * * *

Lord Roseworth hurried away from London immediately after his last interview with Edith Everest, and then the fashionable world began to prick up its ears. There had evidently been some misunderstanding between the young people; perhaps the engagement was really broken off. At last the true story crept out little by little, and was soon whispered over London. Edith Everest became a heroine. No one was tired of praising her.

Yes, there was just one person to whom all this business was a dreadful shock. Aunt Rachel took it very much to heart, and the consequence was that her nervous system was completely shattered. There was nothing she dreaded so much as being talked about, and now her name would undoubtedly be mixed up in the story of her niece's love affairs. She died suddenly at her house in Rutland Gate, within ten days of the great explanation. So sudden and unexpected, indeed, was her death, that the will was never altered; and so Edith Everest was an heiress after all.

   *   *   *   *   *

A boat is gently gliding down the stream, under the woods, by Mapledurham. Two ladies are sitting in the stern, one of them laughing merrily, the other looking earnestly into the happy face of the rower. We have seen them all before. On they go, and the young girl's silvery laugh is still heard as the sound of the oars dies away in the distance. And now the boat stops at a lawn which slopes towards the water. It is Riverside.

THE END.

THE END.

I woke up with a start, and found my father, the Reverend Dewhurst, Mr. Strongitharm, and Bob standing by my bedside. The Bunch of Keys were in the same place where I had seen them before I went to sleep, at the end of the rope hung opposite my bed.

Father looked very grave, and carried in his hand a small switch. I noticed this, because it was not his habit to walk about with a stick or a whip.

"Get up, sir," said father. "A nice chase you have given us!"

"And what a sad amount of unnecessary anxiety!" said the Reverend Dewhurst. "Poor Martha! I thought she would have died when she found that you had gone."

"We'll settle all about that presently," said father.

"Ay, ay, sir; that's right," chimed in Mr. Strongitharm.

I began to cry.

"It's no use crying," said father.

"Not a bit," chimed in Mr. Strongitharm.

"Get up, and dress yourself at once."

I rose and put on my stockings in the lowest possible spirits.

"And now, Dewhurst," said father, "if before this bad boy is quite dressed, you will take Robert for a walk."

"Quite right," said the Reverend Dewhurst. Oh! he was a severe one, he was!

"And if you, Mr. Strongitharm, will kindly excuse us for five minutes."

"Pleasure, sir, take longer if you wish it; make yourself quite at home. You'll find a rope's end there, sir," and Mr. Strongitharm pointed to the rope from which depended the Bunch of Keys.

And I had considered him a friend!

I looked at Bob, who looked at me, and seemed loth to go. The Rev. Dewhurst took him by the hand, but at the door Bob disengaged himself, and coming up to father said—

"Please, father, don't beat Stephen; it was my fault more than his—it was, indeed!"

Father looked at Mr. Dewhurst, who looked back at him; and then they both looked at the light-keeper, who looked back at them. Father stooped and kissed Bob's forehead, and said—

"You go with Mr. Dewhurst, Robert, like a good boy."

And the three left the room.

When father and I were left alone—— But I will pass over what occurred when father and I were left alone, as uninteresting to the general reader and painful to me.

Bob and I were taken home, but not to stay there long. We soon departed for a great house, far, far from Amy, with whom I still correspond through the medium of a sympathetic housemaid. Father had won his Chancery suit, and, as he said, had got his own at last. We—that is, Bob and I—are to pass a year at the Reverend Dewhurst's—oh, happiness! oh, bliss! oh, joy!—and then we go to Eton.

Father often writes to Mr. Strongitharm, who gets somebody to write back for him.

Nothing has transpired to clear up the mystery of the Bunch of Keys, and whether mad old Tilson or anybody else threw them into the stream, or how they came there, is not known to this day, and most likely never will be.

THE END.

HARRILD, PRINTER, LONDON.

NEW AND RECENT WORKS
PUBLISHED BY GROOMBRIDGE & SONS.

Handsomely bound, cloth gilt, with 14 full-page Illustrations, price 5s.,

THE TEMPLE ANECDOTES.
FIRST VOLUME.
ANECDOTES OF INVENTION AND DISCOVERY.
By RALPH AND CHANDOS TEMPLE.

Crown 8vo, with Frontispiece and Vignette, price 6s.,

A BUNCH OF KEYS;
WHERE THEY WERE FOUND, AND WHAT THEY MIGHT HAVE UNLOCKED.
A CHRISTMAS BOOK.
EDITED BY THOMAS HOOD.

CONTENTS:

A Bunch of Keys.—The Ring. By T. W. Robertson.
The Key of the Piano. By T. Archer. | The Key of the Nursery Cupboard. By T. Hood.
The Key of the Strong-Room. By W. S. Gilbert. | The Key of the Study. W. J. Prowse.
Three Keys on a Small Ring of their Own. By C. W. Scott.

NEW WORK BY "THE OLD BUSHMAN."
Nearly ready,

TEN YEARS IN SWEDEN,

An Account of the Geography, Climate, and Field Sports of Scandinavia; together with a Complete List of every Quadruped, Bird, Fish, and Reptile met with at the present day in Sweden, Norway, Finland, and Denmark, with Short Descriptions and Notices of the Habits as well as the Localities frequented by the different Species.

By AN OLD BUSHMAN,

Author of "Bush Wanderings in Australia," "A Spring and Summer in Lapland," etc.

GROOMBRIDGE & SONS, 5, Paternoster Row.

THE OLD BUSHMAN IN LAPLAND.

Post 8vo, cloth gilt, price 10s. 6d.,

A SPRING AND SUMMER IN LAPLAND,
WITH NOTES ON THE FAUNA AND LANDSCAPE OF LULEÄ LAPMARK.

By AN OLD BUSHMAN.

"The book abounds with illustrative anecdotes, incidents of northern travel, the Author's account of his being lost in the snow, and many other details of his experiences, render the Old Bushman's work thoroughly worth reading."—*Athenæum*.

Fcap. 8vo, printed on toned paper, with 36 Initial Letters, and other Illustrations, cloth gilt antique, price 5s.,

THE WARS OF WAPSBURGH.
BY THE AUTHOR OF "THE HEIR OF REDCLYFFE," ETC., ETC.

NEW HISTORICAL CHRISTMAS GIFT-BOOK.

Fcap. 8vo, cloth gilt, with Frontispiece, Engraved by Dalziel,

ROYAL CHILDREN.
THE CHILDHOOD AND SCHOOLROOM HOURS OF ROYAL CHILDREN.

BY JULIA LUARD.

PLAYS FOR HOME ACTING AND YOUNG PERFORMERS.

By JULIA CORNER.

THE KING AND THE TROUBADOUR. A Play for Home Acting and Young Performers. With a Coloured Frontispiece and other Illustrations. Imp. 16mo, gilt edges, 1s.

SLEEPING BEAUTY. A Play for Home Acting and Young Performers. With a Coloured Frontispiece and other Illustrations. Imp. 16mo, gilt edges, 1s.

STORY OF ENGLISH COUNTRY LIFE.

At all the Libraries, 2 vols., post 8vo, price 21s.,

DOROTHY DOVEDALE'S TRIALS.
BY THOMAS MILLER,
Author of "Royston Gower," "Lady Jane Grey," etc., etc.

CRITICAL NOTICES.

"A capital sketch of English country life."—*Guardian*.

"The scenes in which the incidents of this tale occur are described in the happiest manner of this true lover of the country. The very 'spirit of the woods' breathes through them, and there is real rest and refreshment to the mind in the pictures drawn."—*Globe*.

"Dorothy herself is a charming picture—so fresh and innocent, trusting and beautiful. The story of her griefs and of her final trial is painful because of the sympathy which her goodness enlists."—*Morning Star*.

GROOMBRIDGE & SONS, 5, Paternoster Row.

Small post 8vo, cloth,

TWO MONTHS IN A LONDON HOSPITAL.

A Personal Narrative.

BY ARNOLD J. COOLEY,

Author of "Cyclopædia of Practical Receipts, Processes, Data, and Collateral Information," etc.

MR. ARCHER'S NEW WORK.

Post 8vo, cloth,

THE PAUPER, THE THIEF, AND THE CONVICT.

BY THOMAS ARCHER,

Author of "Wayfe Summers," "Madame Prudence," etc., etc.

MR. JOHN HOLLINGSHEAD'S NEW WORK.

Two vols., post 8vo,

TO-DAY.

ESSAYS AND MISCELLANIES.

BY JOHN HOLLINGSHEAD,

Author of "Under Bow Bells," "Odd Journeys," etc., etc.

VOL. I. DAY THOUGHTS.   VOL. II. NIGHT THOUGHTS.

Post 8vo, cloth, gilt, 5s.,

ENGLAND'S WORKSHOPS.

METAL WORKSHOPS—CHEMICAL WORKSHOPS—GLASS WORKSHOPS—PROVISION AND SUPPLY WORKSHOPS—DOMESTIC WORKSHOPS.

MR. MORIER EVANS' NEW WORK.

Post 8vo, cloth, price 10s. 6d.,

SPECULATIVE NOTES,

AND

NOTES ON SPECULATION.

BY D. MORIER EVANS,

Author of "Facts, Failures, and Frauds," "History of the Commercial Crisis," etc.

GROOMBRIDGE & SONS, 5, Paternoster Row.

GIFT BOOKS FOR THE YOUNG.

THE HISTORY OF A SHIP,
From Her Cradle to Her Grave. By GRANDPA BEN. Illustrated with more than One Hundred Engravings. Imperial 16mo, cloth gilt, 3s.

‚ A most attractive book for boys is "The History of a Ship from Her Cradle to Her Grave." A perfect description of a Ship in all her parts, from the keel to the topsail—a book to be read and remembered, written by an author skilled in nautical matters, well read in nautical history, and deeply acquainted with the life of a sailor.

VESSELS AND VOYAGES.
A Book for Boys. By UNCLE GEORGE. Illustrated with Twenty Engravings. 16mo, cloth gilt, 1s. 6d.

OUT AND ABOUT.
A Boy's Adventures. By HAIN FRISWELL, Author of "Footsteps to Fame." Illustrated by GEORGE CRUIKSHANK. Fcap. 8vo, cloth gilt, 3s. 6d.

CHRONICLES OF AN OLD OAK;
Or, Sketches of English Life and History. By EMILY TAYLOR, Author of "The Boy and the Birds," etc. With Full-page Illustrations and Vignettes. Imp. 16mo, cloth gilt, 3s. 6d.

CHILDREN OF OTHER LANDS.
Some Playtime Tales for Children of England. By SARA WOOD. Illustrated with Frontispiece and Vignettes. Imp. 16mo, cloth gilt, 3s. 6d.

CHEAP SERIES OF POPULAR BOOKS.
Price 2s. 6d. each.

UNDER BOW BELLS: a City Book for all Readers. By JOHN HOLLINGSHEAD. Price Half-a-Crown.

ODD JOURNEYS. By JOHN HOLLINGSHEAD. Price Half-a-Crown.

WAYS OF LIFE. By JOHN HOLLINGSHEAD. Price Half-a-Crown.

UNDERGROUND LONDON. By JOHN HOLLINGSHEAD. Price Half-a-Crown.

SELF AND SELF-SACRIFICE; or, Nelly's Story. By ANNA LISLE. Price Half-a-Crown.

ALMOST; or, Crooked Ways. By ANNA LISLE. Price Half-a-Crown.

QUICKSANDS. A Tale. By ANNA LISLE. Price Half-a-Crown.

PICTURES IN A MIRROR. By W. MOY THOMAS. Price Half-a-Crown.

LYDIA: A Woman's Book. By Mrs. NEWTON CROSLAND. Price Half-a-Crown.

A FEW OUT OF THOUSANDS: their Sayings and Doings. By AUGUSTA JOHNSTONE. Price Half-a-Crown.

FOOTSTEPS TO FAME: A Book to Open other Books. By HAIN FRISWELL. Price Half-a-Crown.

LEAVES FROM A FAMILY JOURNAL. By EMILE SOUVESTRE. Price Half-a-Crown.

GROOMBRIDGE & SONS, 5, Paternoster Row.

Price 2s. 6d., each Volume Illustrated with full-page Engravings and Vignettes, appropriately bound in magenta cloth gilt—for PRESENTATION.

THE MAGNET STORIES,
FOR
SUMMER DAYS AND WINTER NIGHTS.
COMPLETE IN EIGHT VOLUMES,
Each Volume containing Seven Original Stories.

CONTENTS OF THE FIRST VOLUME.
When we were Young. By the Author of "A Trap to Catch a Sunbeam."
Lottie's Half-Sovereign. By Mrs. Russell Gray.
Mamma Milly. By Mrs. S. C. Hall.
Havering Hall. By G. E. Sargent.
Blind Ursula. By Mrs. Webb (Author of "Naomi").
The Clockmaker of Lyons. By E. M. Piper.
The Mice at Play. By the Author of "The Heir of Redclyffe."

CONTENTS OF THE SECOND VOLUME.
Union Jack. By Mrs. S. C. Hall.
The Captive's Daughter. By W. Heard Hillyard.
Dear Charlotte's Boys. By Emily Taylor.
The Town of Toys. By Sara Wood.
Not Clever. By Frances M. Wilbraham.
Sea-Shell Island. By G. E. Sargent.
The Pedlar's Hoard. By Mark Lemon.

CONTENTS OF THE THIRD VOLUME.
The Story of Nelson. By W. H. G. Kingston.
Lost in the Wood. By Mrs. Alex. Gilchrist.
The Shepherd Lord. By Julia Corner.
Cousin Davis's Wards. By Margaret Howitt.
Hope Deferred. By Sara Wood.
Which was the Bravest? By L. A. Hall.
The Strayed Falcon. By the Author of "The Heir of Redclyffe," etc.

CONTENTS OF THE FOURTH VOLUME.
The Angel Unawares. By Mary Howitt.
The Little Trapper. By W. Heard Hillyard.
Music from the Mountains. By Mrs. Russell Gray.
Hereward the Brave. By Julia Corner.
Deaf and Dumb. By Mrs. Webb (Author of "Naomi").
An Adventure on the Black Mountain. By F. M. Wilbraham.
No-Man's Land. By Thomas Miller.

CONTENTS OF THE FIFTH VOLUME.
Coraline. By the Author of "A Trap to Catch a Sunbeam."
The Orphans of Elfholm. By Frances Browne.
The Story of a Pebble. By L. A. Hall.
The Sea Spleenwort. By the Author of "The Heir of Redclyffe," etc., etc.
The Christmas Rose. By H. J. Wood.
Ellis Gordon of Bolton Farm. By Emily Taylor.
The Grateful Indian. By W. H. G. Kingston.

CONTENTS OF THE SIXTH VOLUME.
Fanny's Fancies. By Mrs. S. C. Hall.
Sweet Spring Time. By Thos. Miller.
Caldas, a Story of Stonehenge. By Julia Corner.
The Poor Cousin. By Frances Browne.
The Planter's Son. By W. Heard Hillyard.
The Merivales. By Sara Wood.
Peter Drake's Dream. By Francis Freeling Broderip.

CONTENTS OF THE SEVENTH VOLUME.
Golden Autumn. By Thomas Miller.
My Longest Walk. By Mrs. Russell Gray.
The Young Foresters. By Frances Browne.
Helena's Duties. By the Author of "A Trap to Catch a Sunbeam."
Margie's Remembrances. By F. M. Peard.
Purples and Blues. By Emily Taylor.
The Exiles of Berezov. By Frances M. Wilbraham.

CONTENTS OF THE EIGHTH VOLUME.
The Boatswain's Son. By W. H. G. Kingston.
My Life in the Prairie. By Mrs. Webb (Author of "Naomi").
Willy and Lucy. By G. E. Sargent.
Prejudice Lost and Love Won. By L. A. Hall.
Wee Maggie. By Frances F. Broderip.
Wallace, the Hero of Scotland. By Julia Corner.
Rainbow's Rest. By Thomas Hood.

*** Each Volume is bound in an elegant manner, forming a distinct and handsome Gift Book. The Eight Volumes contain 56 Stories, either of which may be had separately, price 3d. each.

GROOMBRIDGE & SONS, 5, Paternoster Row.

Fcap. 8vo, cloth, price 4s., with Illustrative Woodcuts,

A DICTIONARY OF BOTANICAL TERMS.
By the Rev. J. S. HENSLOW, M.A.,
Late Professor of Botany in the University of Cambridge.

Crown 8vo, with 117 Illustrations, cloth gilt, 5s.,

WAYSIDE WEEDS;
Botanical Lessons from the Lanes and Hedgerows.
BY SPENCER THOMSON, M.D.,
Author of "The Structure and Functions of the Eye," etc., etc.

"'Wayside Weeds' is a capital book, and ought to be in every tourist's pocket. We heartily recommend it to those students at Harrow who have just published the result of their well-chosen explorations."—*Reader.*

Eighth Edition, fcap. 8vo, cloth, price 2s. 3d.,

SUGGESTIVE HINTS
TOWARDS IMPROVED SECULAR INSTRUCTION.

Making it bear upon Practical Life. Intended for the use of Schoolmasters and Teachers in our Elementary Schools, for those engaged in the Private Instruction of Children at Home, and for others taking an interest in National Education.

BY RICHARD DAWES, A.M., Dean of Hereford.

Third Edition, fcap. 8vo, cloth, price 2s.,

LESSONS
ON THE PHENOMENA OF INDUSTRIAL LIFE,
AND THE CONDITIONS OF INDUSTRIAL SUCCESS.

Edited by RICHARD DAWES, A.M., Dean of Hereford

Valuable Aid to Composition. Small post 8vo, price 3s. 6d., cloth,

THE DESK-BOOK OF ENGLISH SYNONYMES,
Designed to afford assistance in Composition, and also as a work of Reference, requisite for the Secretary and useful to the student.

BY JOHN SHERER.

"From the very careful and complete manner in which the author has got up his Analytical Index, we should think the volume would readily serve every purpose intended."—*Reader.*
"The object is well carried out."—*Notes and Queries.*
"Abounds in the illustrations of terms, and their many curious affinities."—*Messenger.*
"A very valuable help to the art of composition, as well as a useful book of reference to the secretary and student. Besides the etymology of words we find their general acceptation also explained. An analytical index, containing the whole of the Synonymes, indicated by the pages where they occur, arranged in alphabetical order, facilitates the search for a required word."—*Public Opinion.*

GROOMBRIDGE & SONS, 5, Paternoster Row.

DR. COBBOLD'S NEW WORK ON PARASITES.

In One handsome Volume, super royal 8vo, 508 pages, with Illustrations in Colours and Tints, and numerous Engravings on Wood, price £1 11s. 6d.

ENTOZOA:
AN INTRODUCTION TO THE STUDY OF HELMINTHOLOGY,
WITH REFERENCE MORE PARTICULARLY TO
THE INTERNAL PARASITES OF MAN.

With Twenty-one Coloured and Tinted Plates, comprising One Hundred and Fifty-six separate Figures, together with Eighty-two Woodcuts, making a total of Two Hundred and Thirty-eight Illustrations.

By T. SPENCER COBBOLD, M.D., F.R.S.,
Lecturer on Comparative Anatomy at the Middlesex Hospital.

"A noble contribution to Medical Science which does honour to its author, and is a credit to our national literature. It is the genuine result of continuous and patient research, of great acumen, long literary labour, and honourable devotion to science. The illustrations are numerous, original, and remarkable for their accuracy and beauty. The Publisher has spared no pains in presenting the book in a worthy and splendid dress, the paper and typography are luxurious." —*Lancet.*

Crown 8vo, with numerous Illustrations, price 6s.,

THE UTILIZATION OF MINUTE LIFE.
Being Practical Studies on Insects, Crustacea, Mollusca, Worms, Polyps, Infusoria, and Sponges.

By DR. T. L. PHIPSON, F.C.S.

"There is not a chapter in the work that does not contain numerous facts in natural history on which fortunes have been and might be built."—*Notes and Queries.*

Sixth Edition, price 1s., cloth gilt,

THE BEE-KEEPER'S MANUAL.
Practical Hints on the Management and Complete Preservation of the Honey-Bee.

By HENRY TAYLOR.
Illustrated with One Hundred Engravings.

Crown 8vo, with numerous Illustrations, cloth gilt, 5s.,

THE ROSE BOOK.
A Practical Treatise on the Culture of the Rose, comprising the Formation of the Rosarium, the Characters of Species and Varieties, Modes of Propagating, Planting, Pruning, Training and Preparing for Exhibition, and the Management of Roses in all Seasons.

By SHIRLEY HIBBERD, F.R.H.S.,
Author of "Rustic Adornments," "Profitable Gardening," "Book of the Aquarium," etc., etc.

Post 8vo, cloth, price 3s. 6d.,

PROFITABLE GARDENING.
A Practical Guide to the Culture of Vegetables, Fruits, and other useful outdoor Garden Products; intended for the Use of Amateurs, Gentlemen's Gardeners, Allottees, and Growers for Market.

By SHIRLEY HIBBERD, F.R.H.S.

GROOMBRIDGE & SONS, 5, Paternoster Row.

GRACE AGUILAR'S WORKS.

HOME INFLUENCE. A Tale for Mothers and Daughters. Fcap. 8vo, Illustrated, cloth gilt, 5s.

THE MOTHER'S RECOMPENSE. A Sequel to Home Influence. With a Portrait of the Author, and other Illustrations, fcap. 8vo, cloth gilt, 6s.

WOMAN'S FRIENDSHIP. A Story of Domestic Life. Fcap. 8vo, Illustrated, cloth gilt, 5s.

THE VALE OF CEDARS; or, The Martyr. Fcap. 8vo, Illustrated, cloth gilt, 5s.

THE DAYS OF BRUCE. A Story from Scottish History. Fcap. 8vo, Illustrated, cloth gilt, 6s.

HOME SCENES AND HEART STUDIES. Tales. Fcap. 8vo, with Frontispiece, cloth gilt, 5s.

THE WOMEN OF ISRAEL. Characters and Sketches from the Holy Scriptures. 2 vols., fcap. 8vo, cloth gilt, 10s.

Imperial 16mo, cloth gilt, with Illustrations in Colours, price 7s. 6d.,

TELESCOPE TEACHINGS.

A Familiar Sketch of Astronomical Discovery, combining a Special Notice of Objects coming within the range of a Small Telescope.

By the Hon. Mrs. WARD.

Dedicated, by permission, to the Earl of Rosse.

Illustrated with Coloured Plates, cloth gilt, price 7s. 6d.,

MICROSCOPE TEACHINGS.

Illustrated by the Author's Original Drawings. With Directions for the Arrangement of a Microscope, and the Collection and Mounting of Objects.

By the Hon. Mrs. WARD, Author of "Telescope Teachings."

Second Edition, revised and enlarged, small 8vo, cloth, 3s. 6d.,

OBJECTS FOR THE MICROSCOPE.

A Popular Description of the most Instructive and Beautiful Subjects for Exhibition.

By L. LANE CLARKE.

Post 8vo, Illustrated with Seven Full-page Plates in Tints, and Sixty-five Engravings on Wood, price 5s.,

MARVELS OF POND-LIFE:

Or, A Year's Microscopic Recreations among the Polyps, Infusoria, Rotifers, Water Bears, and Polyzoa.

By HENRY J. SLACK, F.G.S.,

Member of the Microscopical Society of London.

"Messrs. Groombridge have already issued many popular and excellent treatises on some most interesting points of science. Mr. Slack's 'Marvels of Pond Life' will take a worthy place in the series."—*London Review.*

"Mr. Slack has illustrated his remarks with woodcuts, and several very beautifully-executed plates accompany the objects he describes. We recommend Mr. Slack's volume, and express our welcome at the heartiness with which he enters into microscopical work, and the interest he has succeeded in throwing into his researches."—*Quarterly Journal of Microscopical Science.*

GROOMBRIDGE & SONS, 5, Paternoster Row.

I.

Fcap. 8vo, Illustrated, price 5s., with a Memoir of the Author,

HOME INFLUENCE;
A TALE FOR MOTHERS AND DAUGHTERS.
By GRACE AGUILAR.

"Grace Aguilar wrote and spoke as one inspired; she condensed and spiritualized, and all her thoughts and feelings were steeped in the essence of celestial love and truth. To those who really knew Grace Aguilar, all eulogium falls short of her deserts, and she has left a blank in her particular walk of literature, which we never expect to see filled up."—*Pilgrimages to English Shrines, by Mrs. Hall.*

"A clever and interesting tale, corresponding well to its name, illustrating the silent, constant influence of a wise and affectionate parent, over characters the most diverse."—*Christian Lady's Magazine.*

"This interesting volume unquestionably contains many valuable hints on domestic education, much powerful writing, and a *moral* of vast importance."—*Englishwoman's Magazine.*

"It is very pleasant, after reading a book, to speak of it in terms of high commendation. The tale before us is an admirable one, and is executed with taste and ability. The language is beautiful and appropriate; the analysis of character is skilful and varied. The work ought to be in the hands of all who are interested in the proper training of the youthful mind."—*Palladium.*

"In reviewing this work, we hardly know what words in the English language are strong enough to express the admiration we have felt in its perusal."—*Bucks Chronicle.*

"The object and end of the writings of Grace Aguilar were to improve the heart, and to lead her readers to the consideration of higher motives and objects than this world can ever afford."—*Bell's Weekly Messenger.*

"'Home Influence' will not be forgotten by any who have perused it."—*Critic.*

"A well-known and valuable tale."—*Gentleman's Magazine.*

"A work which possesses an extraordinary amount of influence to elevate the mind and educate the heart, by showing that rectitude and virtue conduce no less to material prosperity, and worldly comfort and happiness, than to the satisfaction of the conscience, the approval of the good, and the hope and certainty of bliss hereafter."—*Herts County Press.*

London: GROOMBRIDGE & SONS, 5, Paternoster Row.

GRACE AGUILAR'S WORKS.

II.

THE SEQUEL TO HOME INFLUENCE.

Fcap. 8vo, with a Portrait of the Author and other Illustrations, price 6s.,

THE

MOTHER'S RECOMPENSE;

A SEQUEL TO

"Home Influence, a Tale for Mothers and Daughters."

By GRACE AGUILAR.

"Grace Aguilar belonged to the school of which Maria Edgeworth was the foundress. The design of the book is carried out forcibly and constantly. 'The Home Influences' exercised in earlier years being shown in active germination."—*Atlas.*

"The writings of Grace Aguilar have a charm inseparable from productions in which feeling is combined with intellect; they go directly to the heart. 'Home Influence,' the deservedly popular story to which this is a Sequel, admirably teaches the lesson implied in its name. In the present tale we have the same freshness, earnestness, and zeal—the same spirit of devotion, and love of virtue—the same enthusiasm and sincere religion which characterised that earlier work. We behold the mother now blessed in the love of good and affectionate offspring, who, parents themselves, are, after her example, training *their* children in the way of rectitude and piety."—*Morning Chronicle.*

"This beautiful story was completed when the authoress was little above the age of nineteen, yet it has the sober sense of middle age. There is no age nor sex that will not profit by its perusal, and it will afford as much pleasure as profit to the reader."—*Critic.*

"The same kindly spirit, the same warm charity and fervour of devotion which breathes in every line of that admirable book, 'Home Influence,' will be found adorning and inspiring 'The Mother's Recompense.'"—*Morning Advertiser.*

"The good which she (Grace Aguilar) has effected is acknowledged on all hands, and it cannot be doubted but that the appearance of this volume will increase the usefulness of one who may yet be said to be still speaking to the heart and to the affections of human nature."—*Bell's Messenger.*

"It will be found an interesting supplement, not only to the book to which it specially relates, but to all the writer's other works."—*Gentleman's Magazine.*

"'The Mother's Recompense' forms a fitting close to its predecessor, 'Home Influence.' The results of maternal care are fully developed, its rich rewards are set forth, and its lesson and its moral are powerfully enforced."—*Morning Post.*

"We heartily commend this volume; a better or more useful present to a youthful friend or a young wife could not well be selected."—*Herts County Press.*

London: GROOMBRIDGE & SONS, 5, Paternoster Row.

GRACE AGUILAR'S WORKS.

III.

Fcap. 8vo, Illustrated, price 5s.,

WOMAN'S FRIENDSHIP;

A STORY OF DOMESTIC LIFE.

By GRACE AGUILAR.

" To show us how divine a thing
A woman may be made."—WORDSWORTH.

" This story illustrates, with feeling and power, that beneficial influence which women exercise, in their own quiet way, over characters and events in our every-day life."—*Britannia.*

" The book is one of more than ordinary interest in various ways, and presents an admirable conception of the depths and sincerity of female friendship, as exhibited in England by Englishwomen."—*Weekly Chronicle.*

" We began to read the volume late in the evening; and, although it consists of about 400 pages, our eyes could not close in sleep until we had read the whole. This excellent book should find a place on every drawing-room table—nay, in every library in the kingdom."—*Bucks Chronicle.*

" We congratulate Miss Aguilar on the spirit, motive, and composition of this story. Her aims are eminently moral, and her cause comes recommended by the most beautiful associations. These, connected with the skill here evinced in their development, ensure the success of her labours."—*Illustrated News.*

" As a writer of remarkable grace and delicacy, she devotes herself to the inculcation of the virtues, more especially those which are the peculiar charm of women."—*Critic.*

" It is a book for all classes of readers; and we have no hesitation in saying, that it only requires to be generally known to become exceedingly popular. In our estimation, it has far more attractions than Miss Burney's celebrated, but over-estimated, novel of ' Cecilia.'"—*Herts County Press.*

"This very interesting and agreeable tale has remained longer without notice on our part than we could have desired; but we would now endeavour to make amends for the delay, by assuring our readers that it is a most ably-written publication, full of the nicest points of information and utility that could have been by any possibility constructed; and as a proof of its value, it may suffice to say, that it has been taken from our table again and again by several individuals, from the recommendation of those who had already perused it, and so prevented our giving an earlier attention to its manifold claims for favourable criticism. It is peculiarly adapted for the young, and wherever it goes will be received with gratification, and command very extensive approbation."—*Bell's Weekly Messenger.*

" This is a handsome volume; just such a book as we would expect to find among the volumes composing a lady's library. Its interior corresponds with its exterior; it is a most fascinating tale, full of noble and just sentiments."—*Palladium.*

London: GROOMBRIDGE & SONS, 5, Paternoster Row.

GRACE AGUILAR'S WORKS.

IV.

Fcap. 8vo, Illustrated, price 5s.,

THE VALE OF CEDARS;

OR,

The Martyr.

A STORY OF SPAIN IN THE FIFTEENTH CENTURY.

By GRACE AGUILAR.

"The authoress of this most fascinating volume has selected for her field one of the most remarkable eras in modern history—the reigns of Ferdinand and Isabella. The tale turns on the extraordinary extent to which concealed Judaism had gained footing at that period in Spain. It is marked by much power of description, and by a woman's delicacy of touch, and it will add to its writer's well-earned reputation."—*Eclectic Review.*

"The scene of this interesting tale is laid during the reign of Ferdinand and Isabella. The Vale of Cedars is the retreat of a Jewish family, compelled by persecution to perform their religious rites with the utmost secrecy. On the singular position of this fated race in the most Catholic land of Europe, the interest of the tale mainly depends; whilst a few glimpses of the horrors of the terrible Inquisition are afforded the reader, and heighten the interest of the narrative."—*Sharpe's Magazine.*

"Anything which proceeds from the pen of the authoress of this volume is sure to command attention and appreciation. There is so much of delicacy and refinement about her style, and such a faithful delineation of nature in all she attempts, that she has taken her place amongst the highest class of modern writers of fiction. We consider this to be one of Miss Aguilar's best efforts."—*Bell's Weekly Messenger.*

"We heartily commend the work to our readers as one exhibiting, not merely talent, but genius, and a degree of earnestness, fidelity to nature, and artistic grace rarely found."—*Herts County Press.*

"The 'Vale of Cedars' is indeed one of the most touching and interesting stories that have ever issued from the press. There is a life-like reality about it, which is not often observed in works of this nature; while we read it we felt as if we were witnesses of the various scenes it depicts."—*Bucks Chronicle.*

"It is a tale of deep and pure devotion, very touchingly narrated."—*Atlas.*

"The authoress has already received our commendation; her present work is calculated to sustain her reputation."—*Illustrated News.*

"It is indeed a historical romance of a high class. Seeing how steady and yet rapid was her improvement—how rich the promise of her genius—it is impossible to close this notice of her last and best work, without lamenting that the authoress was so untimely snatched from a world she appeared destined, as certainly she was singularly qualified, to adorn and to improve."—*Critic.*

London: GROOMBRIDGE & SONS, 5, Paternoster Row.

GRACE AGUILAR'S WORKS.
V.
Fcap. 8vo, Illustrated with Frontispiece and Vignette, price 6s.,

THE DAYS OF BRUCE;
A Story from Scottish History.
By GRACE AGUILAR.

"We have had an opportunity of observing the interest it awakens in different classes of readers, and in no instance has it failed to rivet attention, and to induce a high estimate of the author's powers. Miss Aguilar was evidently well read in the times of Bruce. It is long since we met with a work which combines so happily the best qualities of historical fiction."—*Eclectic Review.*

"The life of the hero of Bannockburn has furnished matter for innumerable tales in prose and verse, but we have met with no records of that famous era so instructive as 'The Days of Bruce.'"—*Britannia.*

"'The Days of Bruce' was written when, in the vigour of intellectual strength, Grace Aguilar was planning many things, and all for good; it was we know her especial favourite: it is full of deep interest."—*Mrs. S. C. Hall, in Sharpe's Magazine.*

"It is a volume which may be considered as solid history, but is nevertheless entertaining as the most charming novel ever produced by genius. Sir Walter Scott's name as an author would not have been disgraced by it had it appeared on the title-page instead of Grace Aguilar."—*Bucks Chronicle.*

"This deeply interesting romance—a composition of great eloquence, written with practised polish and enthusiastic energy. We are not surprised at the elegance, the warmth, and the pathos with which Grace Aguilar paints love passages; but we are astonished at the fire and accuracy with which she depicts scenes of daring and of death."—*Observer.*

"The tale is well told, the interest warmly sustained throughout, and the delineation of female character is marked by a delicate sense of moral beauty. It is a work that may be confided to the hands of a daughter by her parent."—*Court Journal.*

"Every one who knows the works of this lamented author, must observe that she rises with her subjects. In 'The Days of Bruce' she has thrown herself into the rugged life of the fourteenth century, and has depicted the semi-civilization of the period in a manner that is quite marvellous in a young woman. Grace Aguilar always excelled in her delineation of female characters, while the skill she evinces in the illustration of the historical personages, and her individualization of the imaginary ones, might at once entitle her to a birthplace among historical novelists."—*Ladies' Companion.*

"Her pen was ever devoted to the cause of virtue; and her various publications, exhibiting the beauties and enforcing the practice of the 'tender charities' of domestic life, have, we doubt not, recommended themselves to the hearts of numbers of her countrywomen. The work before us differs from the former publications of its author, inasmuch as it is in fact an historical romance, for this species of writing the high feeling of Grace Aguilar peculiarly fitted her; many of the scenes are very highly wrought; and while it will fix in the reader's mind a truthful idea of the history and style of manners of 'The Days of Bruce,' it will also impress upon him a strong sense of the ability and noble cast of thought which distinguished its lamented author."—*Englishwoman's Magazine.*

London: GROOMBRIDGE & SONS, 5, Paternoster Row.

GRACE AGUILAR'S WORKS.

"We look upon 'The Days of Bruce' as an elegantly-written and interesting romance, and place it by the side of Miss Porter's Scottish Chiefs."—*Gentleman's Magazine.*

"A very pleasing and successful attempt to combine ideal delineation of character with the records of history. Very beautiful and very true are the portraits of the female mind and heart which Grace Aguilar knew how to draw. This is the chief charm of all her writings, and in 'The Days of Bruce' the reader will have the pleasure of viewing this skilful portraiture in the characters of Isoline and Agnes, and Isabella of Buchan."—*Literary Gazette.*

"What a fertile mind was that of Grace Aguilar! What an early development of reflection, of feeling, of taste, of power of invention, of true and earnest eloquence! 'The Days of Bruce' is a composition of her early youth, but full of beauty. Grace Aguilar knew the female heart better than any writer of our day, and in every fiction from her pen we trace the same masterly analysis and development of the motives and feelings of woman's nature. 'The Days of Bruce' possesses also the attractions of an extremely interesting story, that absorbs the attention, and never suffers it to flag till the last page is closed, and then the reader will lay down the volume with regret."—*Critic.*

VI.

Fcap. 8vo, Illustrated with Frontispiece, price 5s.,

HOME SCENES & HEART STUDIES

Tales.

By GRACE AGUILAR.

The Perez Family.
The Stone-cutter's Boy of Possagno.
Amete and Yafeh.
The Fugitive.
The Edict; a Tale of 1492.
The Escape; a Tale of 1755.
Red Rose Villa.
Gonzalvo's Daughter.
The Authoress.
Helon.
Lucy.
The Spirit's Entreaty.
Idalie.
Lady Gresham's Fete.
The Group of Sculpture.
The Spirit of Night.
Recollections of a Rambler.
Cast thy Bread upon the Waters.
The Triumph of Love.

London: GROOMBRIDGE & SONS, 5, Paternoster Row.

GRACE AGUILAR'S WORKS.

VII.

Second Edition, in Two Volumes, Foolscap 8vo, price 10s.,

THE WOMEN OF ISRAEL;

Or, Characters and Sketches from the Holy Scriptures, illustrative of the past History, present Duties, and future Destiny of Hebrew Females, as based on the Word of God.

By GRACE AGUILAR.

Principal Contents of the Work.

FIRST PERIOD—WIVES OF THE PATRIARCHS.

- Eve.
- Sarah.
- Rebekah.
- Leah and Rachel.

SECOND PERIOD—THE EXODUS AND THE LAW.

- Egyptian Captivity, and Jochebed.
- The Exodus—Mothers of Israel.
- Laws for Wives in Israel.
- Laws for Widows and Daughters in Israel.
- Maid Servants in Israel, and other Laws.

THIRD PERIOD—BETWEEN THE DELIVERY OF THE LAW AND THE MONARCHY.

- Miriam.
- Tabernacle Workers—Caleb's [Daughter.
- Deborah.
- Wife of Manoah.
- Naomi.
- Hannah.

FOURTH PERIOD—THE MONARCHY.

- Michal.
- Abigail.
- Wise Woman of Tekoah.
- Woman of Abel.
- Rispah.
- Prophet's Widow.
- The Shunamite.
- Little Israelitish Maid.

Huldah.

FIFTH PERIOD—BABYLONIAN CAPTIVITY.

- The Captivity.
- Review of Book of Ezra.
- Suggestions as to the Identity of the Ahasuerus of Scripture.
- Esther.
- Review of Events narrated in Ezra and Nehemiah.

SIXTH PERIOD—CONTINUANCE OF THE SECOND TEMPLE.

- Review of Jewish History, from the Return from Babylon to the Appeal of Hyrcanus and Aristobulus to Pompey.
- Jewish History from the Appeal to Pompey to the Death of Herod.
- Jewish History from the Death of Herod to the War.
- The Martyr Mother.
- Alexandra.
- Mariamne.
- Salome.
- Helena.
- Berenice.

SEVENTH PERIOD—WOMEN OF ISRAEL IN THE PRESENT AS INFLUENCED BY THE PAST.

- The War and Dispersion.
- Thoughts on the Talmud.
- Talmudic Ordinances & Tales.
- Effects of Dispersion and Persecution.
- General Remarks.

"A work that is sufficient of itself to create and crown a reputation."—*Pilgrimages to English Shrines, by Mrs. S. C. Hall.*

London: GROOMBRIDGE & SONS, 5, Paternoster Row.

GRACE AGUILAR'S WORKS.

NEW EDITIONS, ILLUSTRATED.

I.
HOME INFLUENCE.
A TALE FOR MOTHERS AND DAUGHTERS.
Fcap. 8vo, Illustrated, Price 5s.

II.
THE MOTHER'S RECOMPENSE.
A SEQUEL TO "HOME INFLUENCE."
Fcap. 8vo, Illustrated, Price 6s.

III.
WOMAN'S FRIENDSHIP.
A STORY OF DOMESTIC LIFE.
Fcap. 8vo, Illustrated, Price 5s.

IV.
THE VALE OF CEDARS.
A STORY OF SPAIN IN THE 15th CENTURY.
Fcap. 8vo, Illustrated, Price 5s.

V.
THE DAYS OF BRUCE.
A STORY FROM SCOTTISH HISTORY.
Fcap. 8vo, Illustrated, Price 6s.

VI.
HOME SCENES AND HEART STUDIES.
TALES.
Fcap. 8vo, Illustrated, Price 5s.

VII.
THE WOMEN OF ISRAEL.
Two Vols., fcap. 8vo, Price 10s.

London: GROOMBRIDGE & SONS, 5, Paternoster Row.

www.ingramcontent.com/pod-product-compliance
Lightning Source LLC
Chambersburg PA
CBHW030740230426
43667CB00007B/785